A Gathering of Witches: Sorcerous Folktales & Curious Accounts

Copyright © 2025 by Roger J. Horne. All rights reserved. First Edition.

No part of this book may be used or reproduced in any manner whatsoever without the written permission of the copyright holder.

ISBN 978-1-7367625-7-8
Moon Over the Mountain Press

A Gathering *of* Witches:

Sorcerous Folktales & Curious Accounts

Retold *by*
Roger J. Horne

Also by Roger J. Horne:

The Charmer's Root: Witching Ways with Common Flora

The Witches' Devil: Myth and Lore for Modern Cunning

A Broom at Midnight: 13 Gates of Witchcraft by Spirit Flight

The Witch's Art of Incantation: Spoken Charms, Spells, & Curses in Folk Witchcraft

Cartomancy in Folk Witchcraft: Playing Cards and Marseille Tarot in Divination, Magic, & Lore

Folk Witchcraft: A Guide to Lore, Land, & the Familiar Spirit for the Solitary Practitioner

Contents

Introduction 1
The Witch of Fife (Scotland) 10
The Witch-Horse (Ireland) 19
The Devil's Garden (New World) 24
A Hand of Glory (England) 29
The Red Book (Scotland) 33
The Witches' Well (Wales) 38
Through Thick and Thin (New World) 43
The Spelled Left Eye (Cornwall) 46
The Broom-Wives (Scotland) 52
The Drowned Suitors (Isle of Man) 58
The Seventh Witch (New World) 61
Nine Witch-Knots (Scotland) 69
The Horned Women (Ireland) 73
The Witch's Bit (New World) 79
The Blighted Orchard (England) 81
The Burning Peat (Scotland) 84
The Nail-Stuck Heart (Wales) 87
The Old Stone Road (New World) 90
The Devil's Yarn (Cornwall) 94
The Black Crane (Scotland) 99
Besom and Crossroads (Isle of Man) 103
The Witch-Wood Charm (New World) 105
Black Paternosters (Scotland) 107

Witch's Legs (Ireland) ... 109
Granny Cobb (New World) ... 113
Milk and Feathers (England) ... 116
Three Knots of Wind (Scotland) ... 118
A Witch-Hare (Wales) ... 120
Devil Take Me, Ring and All (New World) ... 123
The Witch of Treva (Cornwall) ... 127
The Cursing Bone (Scotland) ... 130
The Burning Cauldron (Isle of Man) ... 132
Pins and Pig Livers (New World) ... 134
To Ride the Devil (Scotland) ... 137
Cap and Rue (Ireland) ... 141
The Bent Needle (New World) ... 145
The Wart Tree (England) ... 147
The Horseshoe (Scotland) ... 150
Churchyard Dirt (Wales) ... 152
The Old Black Cats (New World) ... 155
The Kerrow Witch (Cornwall) ... 160
Elf-Bolts (Scotland) ... 163
The Devil's Den (Isle of Man) ... 167
A Silver Bullet (New World) ... 169
Cats' Paws (Scotland) ... 171
The Buried Sheaf (Ireland) ... 175
The Witch's Mill (New World) ... 177
The Witch's Helper (England) ... 181
A Corpse of Clay (Scotland) ... 189

The Counting Curse (Wales) 193
The Black Calf (New World) 197
The Witch's Sow (Cornwall) 203
Turning the Key (Scotland) 207
A Drink of Ash (Isle of Man) 210
Turn and Spin (New World) 212
The Witch's Creel (Scotland) 218
The Witch's Braid (Ireland) 224
Witch-Tracks (New World) 234
Winter's Imps (England) 236
The Black Sheep (Scotland) 240
A Binding Horn (Wales) 243
The Witch-Deer (New World) 246
Whitethorn and Crossroads (Cornwall) 248
A Witch's Promise (Scotland) 250
Nine Bits of Iron (Isle of Man) 254
Churn and Loom (New World) 256
A Gull-Witch (Scotland) 258
The Staining Curse (Ireland) 260
Hoof to Rail (New World) 265
A Witch's Ladder (England) 268
Yarn and Thread (Scotland) 270
Wool of Red, Wool of Blue (Wales) 272
A Dark Blessing (New World) 275
Hair and Nails (England) 278
A Cold Wind in Hell (Scotland) 280

The Charmer's Daughter (Isle of Man) 284
Going by Night (New World) 287
The Witch-Spelled Cow (Ireland) 290
A Sieve by Sea (Scotland) 292
A Host of Spirits (England) 295
The Fork-Stuck Sieve (New World) 298
The Black Goat (Ireland) 301
The Lock Charm (Scotland) 303
The Bloodied Milk (Isle of Man) 305
The Bell Witch (New World) 308
The Catching Gaze (Ireland) 313
Two Rats at Sea (Scotland) 315
A Coat of Clay (England) 318
The Witch's Stone (Scotland) 322
A Witch-Cat (New World) 324
The Hole Stone (Scotland) 327
The Devil's Bride (New World) 329
Bibliography 339

Introduction

Under the cloak of darkness, while the villagers dream in their beds, the witches are gathering. They are just there, on the old stony hill, in the crumbling chapel ruins, among the tombstones of the old churchyard. They are just there, at the edge of the silent lake, beside the moonlit crossroads, in the dark heart of the witch wood. *They are just there,* says the old lore—which is to say, *hidden in plain sight.* Which is to say, *among us.* Which is to say, *our very own selves.*

When we read the old lore of witchcraft, gazing into its still, black pool, the reflection we see there, lingering just beneath the surface, spells a deep truth: that the figure of the witch, no matter how romanticized or villainized, is a part of our very selves, some old part of us that is wild and free, magical and ancient, and perhaps forgotten. The witch of legend bears a face that is our own, though somewhat changed, a reflection in the black mirror of our dreaming. While the witch of lore is sometimes defined as a hag-like creature of legend, and at other times as a kind of shared nightmare, a historical culprit of mass hysteria, these interpretations are both equally reductive, and reading the old lore for ourselves brings us closer, I believe, to understanding on a personal level the complexity and paradox bound up in the term *witch*.

Folklore encompasses the old tales, songs, beliefs, proverbs, and superstitions that have survived through generations of storytellers, through voices both written and oral. Not all folk*lore* takes the form of the folk*tale*, but it is the tale that is the focus of this book. While any particular instance of a given folktale most certainly has an author—for the teller of the tale will inevitably develop their own way of telling the story—the heart of the folktale usually comes to us from hundreds of years ago. And so, when we sample the flavor of a folktale, we are appreciating something both old and new, unique and traditional at the same time. We are tapping the barrel of one particular distillery, but the spirit that we sample feels somehow familiar. Put another way, we are tasting the bread baked by one baker, yet the loaf was made with a special yeast that is hundreds of years old.

For this reason, all folktales are, in a sense, *retellings*, but the tales in this volume are quite decidedly so, for I have tried to render in the telling something that is distinct, a tale flavored with my own voice. Often, I have combined multiple versions of existing folktales that were in circulation around the same time and place, for as any lover of folklore will tell you, it is nearly impossible to find a folktale that does not exist in several variants simultaneously. At times, I have adapted minor details in order to more clearly convey the story's heart. After all, it is the work of storytellers to carry the heart of the story into a new age, so that it may survive another hundred years or more.

The vast majority of these tales come to us thanks to the efforts of folklorists of the 1800s and early 1900s, though their origins are far older than this. Unfortunately, it is quite impossible to say how old these tales may be; we can read the context clues of the tale in order to feel out for ourselves the approximate age, but even this can be deceiving, for such details have surely evolved over the centuries of retellings. Some of these stories clearly suffered, in the old recorded versions, from unfortunate distractions, either due to the anxiety of the storyteller, who surely felt as if they were being studied under the scholar's microscope during the interview, or due to the interference of those academics of previous ages, who often employed exaggerated dialect in their rendition of a tale in order to make the speaker seem quaint or exotic. Some tales were recorded in such reduced and truncated versions that they barely resembled tales at all anymore, being plucked of all their ornament by circumstance and by the ages, published merely as curious ephemera in old periodicals. Accounting for all of these things is a tricky gambit, and I do not claim to have done so perfectly. When all else fails, my approach has been to try to listen to the heart of the story as it finds me and to follow it as closely as I can, for if all efforts are, in the end, imperfect, we can at the very least carry forward the fire that lies at the heart of the thing.

The old witch lore, even in regions influenced by Celtic peoples, is vast and varied. I have found it useful, however, to think of a few basic categories for these tales. The first of these is the *witch encounter*, which can often take the form of a scary story told by the fire. These tales usually go something like this: "I once knew someone, who knew someone else, who had a neighbor who was walking alone at night, and they saw a strange sight..." These folktales are helpful for understanding how beliefs about the figure of the witch were interpreted and passed along across generations. They also demonstrate the ways the witch was believed to be otherworldly, being both human and inhuman, something *other* in the eyes of the teller.

A second type of tale we might discern is the *witchcraft account*. In this sort of folktale, the speaker recounts an experience, usually several accounts or generations removed, of someone who was the performer or the target of a bit of witchery themselves. It is in this category that we find the old curses, but also the old blessings, cures, and protections. These sorts of tales preserve actual remnants of folk magic, sometimes traditions that have died out in practice and exist now only in folk memory. These tales are, for some, useful in terms of rekindling lost ancestral folk practices and remembering who our ancestors once were.

The third type of witch-tale is the most mysterious and intriguing. I refer to it as the *deific witch*, but we can best think of it as an ancient memory of a witching goddess or sorcerer-god. In these sorts of tales, the conjuror or charmer demonstrates powers beyond those of an ordinary practitioner of witchcraft, often performing wonders. These tales often lack all sense of time or place, existing in a kind of dream realm. These figures bear a striking resemblance to ancient pagan deities known for their magical skill, including the Cailleach, Odin/Woden, Holda, or the various horned spirits, of which there are so many, codified under the title of Devil. Sometimes, the resemblance is not to a traditional deity, per se, but to a faery, or even to a local spirit of a place (genius locus) who would have been known in an ancient age long forgotten, and was possessed of a uniquely sorcerous nature. It is easy to mistake these tales for being reduced or eroded versions of ancient wisdom, to delude ourselves into thinking that the old version would be somehow superior to this one, but we must remember that, in the lore at least, the personage of such spirits evolves quite naturally over time. There exists no singular, eternal, ancient wisdom that has been adulterated over the ages; instead, true wisdom is a living, shifting thing, and if we approach these tales without prejudice and truly listen, we will find in them a wisdom of their own.

Some of the tales in this collection bear a striking resemblance to one another, and that is, of course, no accident. "The Witch of Fife," for example, is incredibly similar to the Irish tale "Cap and Rue." This does not mean, as some might infer, that one version is the originator of the other, for they both probably evolved from the same source, and that source itself was probably a branch of another tree, and so on. Similarly, "The Witch-Horse" has many elements similar to "The Old Stone Road." These jewels of folklore were probably brought to the New World by immigrants, who adapted a new version of the tale that began its circulation there, but we cannot be absolutely certain. All of this is to say, reader, that I hope these similarities are interesting and illuminating, and not a cause for pitting one tale against another, as if we were trying to find the "true" or "best" version of such stories, for folklore is like a hall of mirrors, or perhaps like a dark hallway full of echoes, and such efforts are a distraction from the real treasures set before us.

The richest trove in these folktales, and in my opinion, the best perspective from which to contemplate them, lies in the subtle threads that run between and across the old stories. Witch lore is like a tapestry, and certain colors of thread seem to rise again and again, forming a pattern. We find the element of secrecy, of the witch who appears ordinary, but is something else underneath, hidden in plain sight, the human body as a kind of costume or vessel to be taken off or abandoned at will. We find flight and animal transformation, both encompassing a kind of yearning to be wild and free and an old folk memory of the animistic practices of otherworldly travel. We find charms, in various iterations, for the manipulation of life force, either of someone's health, or their fertility, or the prosperity of their land. We find the importance of dreams and nightmares, of the ways the witch can bend perception in states of liminal consciousness. We find punishments and rewards, witches who deliver justice based on old codes and customs, often reflecting values that were antiquated even in older times. We find witches defying social norms, practicing heretical versions of the popular faith of their day, performing deeds forbidden to their gender, and eschewing the weakness their society expected of them based on their social class, their heritage, or their sex.

We also find the many tales of what has at times been called *white witchcraft*. Many practitioners, who were very real people, ancestors of some of us who are still living today, offered practical magical services to their communities, whether by the old healing ways, or by protective charms over one's land and one's family, or by divination and augury. And we see in the accounts of the witch trials that these folk were sometimes the targets of witch hunters, while at other times, their services were employed to counteract the supposed workings of witches. Their stories are here, too, in various iterations, but make no mistake: the services offered by "white witches" included darker craft as well—the punishment of thieves and enemies, the silencing of tongues, the cursing of criminals, abusive spouses, and enemies. In some ways, the differentiation between "good" and "evil" witches was itself a stratagem of those practitioners who wished to avoid the noose or the pyre, which was sometimes successful and other times not. Inevitably, we find that the charms of the old "white" and "black" witchcrafts are much the same, relying on similar mechanics and differing mostly in the way the tale is told.

But the most paradoxical discovery that I hope you will make in these old stories is this: that the protagonist of these tales, the one who sees strange things in the forest, the one beset with the curse, who somehow survives by means of their cunning, is made, by the end of the tale, *a witch themselves*. For in order to undo the curse, in order to survive the wicked spirits, in order to find the thing that has been stolen or accomplish whatever the goal may be, the hero must learn some manner of craft of their own, and so the end of one witch-tale is the beginning of another, for the challenge posed by the malevolent witch is nothing if not an initiation, bringing the hero into some new version of themselves, now armed with their own strange magics.

As you make your way through these tales, dear reader, tread gently and kindly. Consider that these stories were told once by friends and neighbors, mothers and fathers, shared with love and with wonder. The old lore is frightening, yes, and it is full of unpleasant things that we may prefer to avoid, but the characters of these tales are also, in a way, the beloved elders of those of us who come from one or more of these places. When we retell these tales, we can feel the old generations with us again, as if their very spirits were conjured by the telling, and while that may sound like a haunted thing to say, it is actually a comfort. Many things that seem haunted are really made of memory and love, and I hope the love in these old collective memories reaches you, reader, and warms your bones on dark nights, beside the glow of your own crackling fire.

The Witch of Fife
Scotland

A very long time ago, there lived an elderly couple who made their home together in the Kingdom of Fife. Although the pair were generally well-regarded, many suspected the wife of being a witch, for she had a cunning way about her and a secretive, impish sort of smile. She spent little time in church, and she could not be commanded to do anything but by her own will.

Even her husband himself suspected her of witchcraft, for his wife would disappear on the night of the new moon, not returning until dawn. When questioned, she would say, "I was merely walking" or "I lost track of time" or some other such nonsense reply, all given with a sly smile. Nor could he ever catch her in the act of leaving; try as he might to be vigilant, his wife would slip away the moment he turned to any task, and by the time he reached the door, she had quite vanished into the darkness and the mist.

In those days, of course, there was a great fear of witches. And there certainly were many who would rather turn their spouse over to the authorities than remain married to a practitioner of the dark arts. But the old man loved his wife with a steadfast and true love, and while he feared to learn the truth of her nocturnal sojourns, he hated more the thought of a secret set between them.

"Good wife," he said to her one night by the warmth of the hearth, "I will not be angry if you tell me the truth. I have loved you since the first day we met. Only tell me at last, are you a witch?"

The old woman placed her hand over his, gazing into the fire, and replied, "I am what you say."

The man took a long drink of whisky to steel himself.

"Each night of the new moon," she continued, "I leave this house to meet with a hidden company I cannot name, and to conduct such business of witchery that I cannot discuss. You must understand. I love you dearly, husband, but such things should not be spoken of."

"All these years we have loved and cared for one another," the old man said, "and you would yet keep secrets from me? You know I would tell not a soul. I would have no harm come to you, no matter how dark your deeds of witchery."

The witch was moved then, and she looked at him warmly. "I do know it, husband. The next new moon, after I return from my journey, I will tell you all that happened. But you must promise not to involve yourself, not to set foot on this path of mine in any way, lest any harm come to you."

And so he promised, and so it was that the old woman embarked again upon the next new moon, disappearing in the night as before, and when she returned with the rising sun, looking quite tired and spent, her husband asked her to relay the tale of her journey.

She told him how she walked to the abandoned ruins of an old church in the countryside, how she met with four other witching folk among the crumbling stones, how they picked stalks of hemlock and transformed them into magical horses that they might ride invisibly through the country with the cold wind in their hair, how they ran with the foxes and flew with the owls, and how they at last came to a great mountaintop to rest and to drink their witch-brew out of horn cups, an ale made not by mortal hands, how the Devil appeared to them as a small man cloaked in shadow, playing such sweet pipe music that the crows and the herons perched nearby to listen, how the witches danced until their legs could dance no more.

The old man was unimpressed by this tale. "All of this magic, and you merely rode, drank beer, and danced a bit? Would you not have been warmer and safer at home?" And with that, he went off to tend the farm.

On the next new moon, the witch went again on her journey and returned at dawn looking quite fatigued. Again the old man asked what had transpired, and again she relayed the tale of her journey.

She told him how this time, the witches had taken cockle-shells and enchanted them with their witchcraft into magical boats, how they had sailed across the cold sea, the pale starlight glinting on the waters and the ocean mist spraying their cheeks, how they came to a faraway shore where gathered many other witches and warlocks, and also faeries of all kinds, mermaids of the sea and phantom hunters of the deep and forbidden forests, brownies and pixies of the old hills, how they all feasted together and danced once again to the Devil's wild pipe music, how the spirits taught them the strange sorcery of undoing locks and breaking chains, of how to gain entry to any place or free oneself from any restraint, how the witches were delighted with this new knowledge and talked giddily their whole journey home.

Once more, the old man was unimpressed. "With all your witchcraft, and all you could do with such power, you merely sailed, ate, and learned a bit of lockpicking? You could have been hurt or worse. Is all this business really worth it?"

"It is no mere lockpicking, husband. You'll see. We've already decided how to use the charm, and next new moon, I'll tell you what prize my witchery has won."

The old man sighed and rubbed his brow, then set off to tend the farm as usual.

The next new moon, his witch wife disappeared once more into the night, and when she returned the next morning, she was again tired, but she was so eager to tell her husband the tale that she could scarcely sit down for a cup of tea. She told him how the witches and warlocks had caught wind of the town bishop's well-stocked wine cellar, full of fine and expensive wines of excellent vintage, how they had gathered at the home of one of the older witches, how they had placed their feet upon the fireplace crook, how they had spoken the secret charm the elves taught them, which immediately whisked them up the chimney and past the locked door of the bishop's wine cellar, how they laughed and sang and drank all night from such excellent wine that few had ever tasted in their lives.

At this, the old man was at last impressed, for he was a great lover of wine, and too poor to afford it but on seldom occasion. "My brilliant wife!" he exclaimed. "If your witchcraft can do this, then it is indeed worth all the risk and the trouble. Take me with you tonight, my love, that I might enjoy the bishop's fine vintage myself."

"I cannot, husband dear," she replied. "This is witch business, and you yourself promised me that you would not get involved. If any harm came to you, it would wound me terribly."

The old man looked utterly defeated then and gazed at the floor.

"It is for the best, my love," she said after a pause.

But the old man had already made up his mind what to do, for he could not bear the thought of such excellent vintage so close within his reach. Besides, he thought, why should I not benefit in some way from my wife's witchery?

And so, the next new moon, he waited outside the window of the eldest witch's cottage, and he watched as they spoke the charm and placed their feet upon the chimney crook to be whisked away to the bishop's wine cellar. After the last of the witches had departed, he went in himself and worked the charm, and to his surprise, it worked for him as well any warlock, as if he were something of a witch himself.

Needless to say, the witches were terribly alarmed when the old man suddenly appeared among their company in the wine cellar. One particularly tall warlock demanded that he leave at once. A younger witch suggested they kill him, lest he tell their secret. But the man's wife, who was a well-known and respected witch among their number, swore him to be a trustworthy man, one true to his word, and at last, they allowed him to stay. And in the course of the evening, after a great deal of wine had been drunk, one would think they had all been friends for ages. They laughed and drank and sang old songs, and the old man had one of the happiest nights of his life.

It was in the early hours of the morning that there came a stern knock at the door, and then the light of a lantern, and then the company could make out the voice of the bishop himself demanding to know who had broken into his wine cellar. At this, the witches all spoke the charm to whisk themselves away into the night, but the old man, having imbibed more than his share of wine, couldn't remember the words, and so the only one the bishop and his men found in the cellar was the old man, drunk and rosy-cheeked, surrounded by empty wine bottles.

"And what, good man, are you doing in my wine cellar?" demanded the bishop.

"Oh...yes...well," replied the old man drunkenly, "I flew here on the wind, by dark sorcery of course, to laugh and sing and drink with the witches!"

Needless to say, the bishop had him taken into custody then, and it was not long before he was charged with witchcraft, and it was not long after that that the entire town believed wholeheartedly that the old man was a warlock himself, dangerous and vile, deserving of the stake. Not once during all of this did the old man name his wife or any other in that company, but kept their secret, for though he had broken his promise to his wife not to get involved in witch-business, he loved her still, and he could not bear the thought of her being harmed.

On the day of his execution, the poor old man was chained and set upon a wooden pyre, and he cried silently as the townsfolk shouted in glee, for he knew there was no hope left and that he would die by fire. The sentence was pronounced, and a man with a torch came to light the pyre in several places. As the smoke stung his eyes, the old man thought of his wife's face, wishing only that he could see her again one more time.

It was then that a strange gray bird appeared in the sky. It flew down through the smoke, landing on the old man's shoulder, and in his wife's own voice, it spoke the incantation for the breaking of chains and flight beyond boundaries. At once, his shackles were broken like glass, and he flew over the crowd of people, who were shocked and terrified at such a sight. The old man flew after the strange gray bird, following it all the way to his own home, where it landed and became his own witch wife, who threw her arms about him and kissed him, laughing and crying all at once.

The two of them lived a long and happy life together, and they were not bothered again by the bishop or the townsfolk, for the people were quite afraid of him after that, thinking him a powerful warlock, wicked and skillful in the dark arts, which was quite the funny thought in the eyes of the wife, who was the true witch of Fife, but she had no desire to correct them.

The Witch-Horse
Ireland

Many ages ago, there lived a very wealthy woman many suspected of being a witch, for her house was always stocked with the choicest food, wine, and fineries, and she was never seen to go anywhere but at night. She took no husband and had no family wealth to explain her luxuries. When asked about the source of her great fortune, she would simply remark, "I have paid the fair price for it all."

Most suspicious of all, she was seen about the countryside at night, riding a different horse each time. On one moonlit night, she would be seen riding a gray one, and another night, a dappled one, but by the naked light of day, there would be no horses in her stables at all. Each time she was seen riding about in the night, another young man would take ill the following morning, often dying soon after, and the townsfolk began to suspect that her witchery was of a particularly dark variety—that of tormenting her victims by riding them about in the form of horses, in order to drain their vitality and their good fortune for herself.

Goodness knows there are many forms of witchery in the world, some helpful and others harmful, but of all the malevolent ones, this was indeed thought to be one of the most fearsome. A witch who could ride her victims had only to place an enchanted item, often a harness or a bit, upon them while sleeping, and such witches could enter any house through chimney or keyhole. None could be truly safe from such dark sorcery. And so folks grew afraid of the woman and kept their distance. They began referring to her as "the lady witch," in reference to her great wealth.

One young man of the village, however, did not believe the rumors for himself, and he wished to get to the bottom of the matter one way or the other. He brought cakes to her home one day, and bread the next, and before long, he had befriended her, though she was quite guarded still, for no matter how much time they spent together, he could not be sure if she was a witch or not. When he brought up the rumors from the townsfolk, she would simply laugh and tell a joke, and when he mentioned anything to do with witches at all, she would merely smile and change the subject. Once, he mentioned yet another young man from the village who had wasted away from the mysterious illness, and though she made no remark, he could swear he saw the faintest wry smile upon her lips as she sipped her tea.

At last, he decided that the only way to come to a clear answer on the matter was to stay the night at her home. He brought several bottles of fine Spanish wine the next evening, and they talked and laughed the hours away, drinking their fill. The young man made sure, though, that he filled the witch's glass more often than he filled his own, sipping only enough to be convincing, and pouring the rest away where it would not be seen so that he seemed to have imbibed his own weight in wine.

He stood to leave at last, and stumbled intentionally, pretending to be quite drunk, and surely enough, his host suggested that he should sleep on the couch until the morning, for he seemed in no shape to be riding home. The young man agreed, and after the lady witch retired to her chamber, he stretched out upon the couch, feigning sleep.

It was not long before he heard footsteps coming down the stairs, and with his one open eye, he saw for himself the lady witch walking calmly towards him with a candle in one hand and a bridle in the other. She set the candle down upon the table, and very slowly and carefully went to place the bridle upon her guest. What a surprise was hers, then, to find that the young man was not asleep at all. He leapt to his feet, and in one swift motion, snatched the bridle from her and threw it upon the lady witch herself.

Her face was furrowed with rage, but only for a moment, for her chin stretched down, and her eyes rolled to the sides of her head, and as quickly as that, she had become a great red mare standing in the middle of her own house. The young man was taken aback for a moment then, for the charm worked as well in his hands as it might in the hands of any witch. "Let us see how you like your own witchery, then!" said the young man, who at once mounted her and rode her out into the cold and moonless night.

The lady witch tried to resist her rider several times. "Release me now, dear boy," she said to him, "and I'll stock your cellar with the finest wines in all the world."

"The Devil take your wine," he replied, and rode on.

"Merely stop for a moment, dear boy," said the witch-horse, "that I might take a drink of water from a stream, and I'll grant you such terrible power that all will fear and obey you."

The young man thought of all the poor boys from the village who had died terribly. "The Devil take your power," he replied, and rode on.

"Please, dear boy," said the witch-horse at last, "my feet are worn, for I am not shod as a real horse would be. Torment me no further."

"Tormented, are you?" replied the young man. "As tormented as those poor souls you've wasted away over the years? Still, I am not without pity. Shod you shall be." And so he took her to a nearby farrier and woke him from his sleep in order to have her properly shod.

When at last the night was nearly spent, he rode her to her own home, and removed the bridle at last, at which she immediately changed back into the form of a woman. Her dress was in tatters, and her face gaunt and pale. Much to both of their surprise, the horseshoes were still upon her hands and feet, nailed into her very flesh, and leaving wounds that rendered her feeble and frail for the rest of her days.

Upon returning home, the young man found that his cabinets were full of gold coins, one coin for every mile that he had ridden the witch-horse, and his larders were full, and his cellar was stocked with fine wine. He lived the rest of his days in comfort, having excellent luck in all of his endeavors, and it was the lady witch herself who paid the fair price for it.

The Devil's Garden
New World

Several generations ago, in the wild hills of Kentucky, there lived a farmer with very little to show for his efforts. His cows produced little milk, his corn withered on the stalk, and his chickens would seldom lay. Times were hard, but not for all, for the farmer noticed that his neighbors all around him always had as much as they needed and enjoyed success in all their endeavors.

On a hot summer evening, the farmer paid a visit to his closest neighbor in the hopes of trading his pig. The sun was red and swollen on the horizon. Crows cried out in nearby cornfields on his journey, and crickets sang with the coming of evening. The farmer wiped the sweat from his brow, and as he traveled along the old dirt road, he prayed to the Lord for an answer to his troubles, a way to save his farm and his family from hunger.

At last, he arrived at his neighbor's cabin, and they welcomed him in and offered him a cold drink, and they were only too happy to trade fairly for the hog. As they sat on the porch, the husband spied a stray goat nearby, and he excused himself so as to fetch it and secure the fence before dark came over the valley. The wife invited their guest inside in the meantime for a bit of bread and butter.

"I've no butter," said the woman, "but that's no matter. I can churn some in but a moment." And as quickly as you please, the woman poured just a bit of cream into her churn, and it grew and grew as she worked it, which only took a few short moments, until the churn was full of more butter than the farmer thought possible.

As she turned to slice the bread, he peeked at the churn, snooping inside and beneath it to solve the mystery, and there on the floor just under the thing was a small red charm bag, embroidered with strange symbols and letters. The farmer quickly snatched it before the woman could see, and he placed it in his pocket for safekeeping.

"I think I'll check on your husband," the farmer said. "He may need help with that goat." But of course, he had no intention of staying a moment longer. He rushed to his horse and wagon and made his way home as quickly as he could.

The cornfields along the old road had gone quiet, and the moon had risen wide and yellow over the hills.

When he reached home, he immediately ran to his wife and explained what he had witnessed at his neighbor's house. At first, she did not believe him, and so she took the red charm bag from him, placed it under her own churn, and poured just a mere splash of cream into it, then began to work the thing. As she churned, the cream grew and grew, and before they could count to ten, it was filled with butter, just as the farmer had witnessed before.

For a moment, the couple believed that their problems were solved, and that the Lord had come to their aid at last, but they had no time to celebrate their fortune, for there came then a loud knock at the door. The man hid the red charm bag in his coat pocket quickly.

When he answered the front door, what he saw filled him with dread. He had suspected it might be his neighbor, come to reclaim the stolen charm, but instead, what stood before him was the tall figure of a man, dressed all in black, and shrouded in darkness such that he could not make out his face, only his eyes, which shone with a pale light as yellow as the moon above.

The tall figure removed its hat and bowed politely, then brought out from his jacket a small book, which looked much like a pocket bible, the kind folks often keep on their person when traveling. The tall man handed it to the farmer then, and upon closer inspection, the farmer found it to be nothing like a bible at all. It was bound in black leather, but with strange markings all over it, filled with old, yellowed pages with fraying edges, and though the night air was hot, the book was as cold as ice in his hands.

"Will you sign?" said the tall man, with a voice like the rustling of wind through dry leaves. The farmer opened the book then, and there inside were written all of the names of his neighbors, of every last neighbor for miles and miles, such that the majority of the county was represented in the man's little book. "Sign, and you shall never hunger," said the man as the farmer thumbed through the pages. "Sign, and you shall never thirst."

The farmer's wife, who had been standing behind him in the doorway this whole time, placed her hand on her husband's shoulder then, and looked into his eyes with fear. *No*, her eyes pleaded.

"You've all but signed already," said the strange man, who then snapped his fingers and held them out before him, and the farmer felt a thrashing in his jacket pocket where he had tucked the red charm bag, and from the pocket flew out a little red bird, which fluttered in the air a bit before landing on the tall man's finger. It looked the farmer and his wife up and down, its eyes as strange and yellow as the man's, and then it began laughing in a ragged human voice, like an old drunk who had been told the best joke of his life.

"All right, then," said the farmer, who proceeded to write in the strange man's book, but instead of signing his name, he wrote the words:

We and all that we possess belong to the Lord.

Upon reading this in his book, the visitor scowled and let out something like a groan, and he turned with his little bird on his shoulder and made his way down the hill, disappearing into the tall rows of corn.

The farmer and his wife moved away shortly after that, for they did not care to live among so many witching folk. None built their house on that plot of land again after that, and to this day, none will. From the spot where the strange man stood grew a thick patch of sage grass, sometimes called broomsedge, and it grew and grew until it covered a whole acre. Some folks called it the Devil's Garden. And that is what it is called to this very day.

A Hand of Glory
England

It was long ago, on a barren moor in Yorkshire, that there once sat a lonely inn, which was owned and managed by a small family. They had but one servant girl who helped them in keeping up with the place by tending to guests, and by cleaning and cooking and such.

One dark night, after the inn had closed its doors and all of the guests and the family had retired for the evening, there came a soft tap at the door. Only the servant girl was still awake, tending to the last of her chores. When she answered, there stood in the doorway a poor beggar man, who was shivering in the cold, his clothes soaked through by a passing storm.

The kind girl welcomed him inside to warm himself by the fire, and he seemed to her a gentle soul down on his luck, and so, although there were no remaining beds at the inn available, she offered him a mat on the floor beside the fire, that he might at least have someplace warm and dry for the night, and then make his way silently out of the inn before the sun rose in the morning, so that none would scold her for letting him inside.

The beggar thanked her graciously and profusely, perhaps with too much feigned sweetness in his tone, for the girl felt instinctively then that there was something strange about this man. In those days, it was known that criminals and witching folk wandered about in this part of the country, and could cause all manner of mischief if one was not vigilant. And so she perched at the top of the stairs and watched him for a while to be sure he was not up to some trouble.

The man lay still for a time, but then, once he was convinced that the entire house was asleep, he reached into his jacket pocket and produced what looked to be a small, withered human hand, its skin yellow and leathered with age, and its fingernails long and thick. The girl held her hand to her mouth to stop herself from gasping in horror. The man then stuck the hideous thing upon a pronged candlestick, anointed each of its fingers with some sort of oil, and lit them, one after another, muttering strange incantations, and the fingertips of the hand caught light by that fire, and they flickered and shone like candles.

The man then stood, his macabre lantern in hand, and the girl rushed up to the bedroom of the man and wife who owned the inn, seeking to wake them, to tell them what she had just seen. They could not be woken, however, but were spelled into a deep sleep that looked like death. It was clear to the girl then that this man was not only a criminal, but a dark magician, and that this withered hand had somehow compelled all of the sleepers in the house not to wake so long as the thing remained lit.

The girl watched from the crack of the door as the dark sorcerer worked his way through the rooms of the inn with a bag, stealing any valuables he could, and the bag grew larger and heavier as he went on, robbing one sleeper after another. She perched behind some furniture as the man entered the room of the husband and wife, and his sack had become so big and heavy that he had to set down the flickering hand for a moment in order to shift its weight.

It was then that the girl snatched the horrible thing, running down the stairs with it as quickly as she could. She tried to blow it out, but its flames did not move, as if they were impervious to wind. She tried throwing it into a pail of water, but the flames continued to burn, even soaked through. She could hear the thief's footsteps approaching closer now, which would surely mean her death, and as a last resort, she poured a bottle of milk over the hand, and at last, its flames fizzled out, and she was able to scream for help, at which all of the guests and the owners came running and apprehended the man.

And the charmed hand used by the sly beggar man that night was called the Hand of Glory, a legendary object made from the hand of a hangman, dried and sealed with wax, said to allow one to walk about unseen, for it compels all others but the wielder to a deep, death-like sleep in one's presence, and to this day it is said that many petty conjurors, especially those inclined to theft and other crimes, treasure this charm above all others.

The Red Book
Scotland

Many are the tales of great and wondrous books of the black art, tomes that grant strange powers to those who can unlock the secrets therein. One such legendary grimoire, known as the Red Book of Appin, was so darkly potent that the witch or warlock who wished to read it had to wear an iron crown upon his head to ward off wicked spirits. For those willing to risk the danger, the book was said to give the charmer power over animals, to cure the afflictions of cattle and to bewitch creatures of the earth in various ways. The tale of its origin is a strange matter indeed.

It is said that there once lived, near the town of Appin, a poor miller's apprentice who longed for a more prosperous future. He had heard from the townsfolk that there gathered upon a nearby rocky hilltop a coven of witches, who were seen to dance and sing about their fire in the company of the Devil. Despite the danger, the apprentice saw no other way to the finery he craved than to embark to the spot and learn what he could from the witches and their master.

The young man was filled with fear as he waited behind a large stone in the dark, but finally, after many cold hours, he saw the mysterious figures arrive at the spot, just as predicted. Once the witches were all gathered around and the fire was lit, a great and cacophonous chanting commenced, and there appeared a long shadow before the fire, and from that shadow stepped the Devil himself. He called the witches forward one by one and seemed to kiss them, until at last he turned his head to stare at the rock behind which the young man was hiding, and announced in a deep, growling voice, "And you, you who would be more than you are, step forward as well."

A cold fear gripped the young apprentice, and though he went pale and his hands trembled, he could do nothing but step forward and reveal himself, as if his body was no longer his own. He stepped forward clumsily towards the gathering of witches, each of them staring and smiling at him, as if they were watching the performance of some pageant they had seen so many times that they knew it all by heart.

"I know the desire in your heart," said the Devil, "the desire to be wealthy and secure in your future, to have fine clothes and a stately home, to never feel hunger or cold again in your mortal life."

"Yes! Yes, that is my desire!" cried the poor miller's apprentice, who was so overcome by his yearning that he no longer trembled with fear.

"Make compact with me, then, and you shall have all that and more," said the Devil, and with that, he presented him a red book gilt with gold. "Take this quill, and sign."

The young man brought the quill to within a hair's breadth of the page, but then stopped himself. "Once I sign, you will own my soul, won't you, sir, and you'll carry me off to Hell when I die? Is that not so?"

The Devil sighed deeply, and a great plume of hot goat-breath mingled with the cold air. "Once you sign, you will belong to God no longer."

The young man remembered then the fiery sermons of his youth, and in a moment of panic, ran as fast as his legs could carry him, not looking back until he reached the edge of town. Though he could spy the hilltop from the distance, there was no fire there at all. It was then he realized that the red book was still in his hands, for he had never cast it aside when he ran away. Shaking with fear, he hid the book beneath his bed and tried to sleep, though he could not.

The next night, after a tiresome day at the mill, the young man heard a deep and frightening voice outside his cottage, saying, "Return to me what is mine." He knew that it must be the Devil, come to claim either the book or his soul—or both. He quickly laid a circle of salt about himself, remembering the old stories in which the Devil could not cross such a boundary.

But the Devil burst into the little cottage, and in a frightening display of power, transformed himself into a pack of greyhounds. They circled the young man, eyes full of rage, growling, snarling, and snapping at the young thief, yet they were unable to cross the circle of salt, and so they could not harm him.

Then the Devil transformed himself into a flock of crows, which flew all around him, darting in and out as if to peck out his eyes and tear at his flesh. But like before, the creatures could not cross the boundary of salt, and so they could not harm the young man.

Before the Devil could attempt a third trick, the sun broke over the hillside, and with the sunrise, Auld Hornie departed at last. The miller's apprentice kept the red book as his secret treasure, and in time, he learned its charms of mastery over beasts, becoming a successful and well-respected expert in all matters to do with the keeping of horses, cattle, and hounds. And his book, stolen from the very Devil, became known after his death as the Red Book of Appin.

The Witches' Well
Wales

In another age, long ago, a great community of witches lived around the village of Llanddona, and they were known in that time for the potency of their curses and the malevolent nature of their craft. How they arrived in the village, and why they were permitted to remain there, is the stuff of legend, indeed.

It is said that they arrived on a boat without oars, which was a common punishment for criminals in those days, who would be shoved off on a vessel into the cruel sea with no means of returning. Such boats, when they came ashore, were always pushed back into the waves, but the witches who landed in Llanddona jumped off swiftly, and by their witchcraft, they conjured a stream of ensorcelled water from the ground, to the delight of all their would-be enemies, and for this, they were allowed to stay there. And in time, that spring became a well, and that well was renowned for its magical potencies.

But despite the occasional act of benevolence in order to appease the people, the witches of Llanddona caused more harm than good. The greatest among their number, who was known as Bella Fawr, would bewitch cows and pigs, crops and hens, and anything else she liked. And so, when the witches of Llanddona came to one's door, it was customary to give them whatever they asked for, be it milk or butter or meat or coin, in order to appease them, for if they detected even the slightest offense, Bella Fawr would lay a curse upon the family, and ruin and disaster would follow.

Now, this went on for some time, the witches threatening whoever they pleased and taking what they wanted from innocent people, but eventually, even the very powerful are sure to make mistakes. And that mistake went by the name of Goronwy Tudor, for old Bella Fawr could think of no time that Goronwy had made any sort of offering to the witches, not of his butter or eggs or anything at all, and so she set her bewitchments upon him as punishment.

Unbeknownst to her, Goronwy Tudor was a conjuror himself, and one of great power, a sorcerer and white witch of the highest caliber. He had been born with a certain birthmark sign over his chest, signifying protection against witcheries. He kept horseshoes nailed above every door and rings of mountain ash at the doorposts. He regularly collected churchyard dirt to sprinkle about his property with his incantations, and so he could not be assaulted by any common witcheries of the usual sort, and old Bella Fawr was greatly vexed, and decided to resort to harsher measures.

Over the next several weeks, she took to tormenting his farm personally by visiting it in the form of a hare, and with this, at last, she was able to achieve success in her black witchcraft. The conjuror detected this immediately, however, and knew just what to do. He took a pail of milk from a bewitched cow that she had been tormenting, and he heated a poker over a fire until it glowed red. As he plunged the thing into the vessel of milk, it steamed and bubbled and hissed, and out flew Bella Fawr in the form of a witch-hare. At this, Goronwy Tudor took up his gun, which he had loaded with a silver coin, and fired.

And the witch-hare returned to her own form then, that of an old woman, blood running down one of her legs from where the silver coin had penetrated her flesh, and the sight of her was a horrifying thing then, for her face was wrenched and twisted in rage, and the very air about her seemed dark and heavy with venomous intent. She rose from the ground, limping on one leg, and escaped into the distance, making her way to the magical well of the witches of Llanddona, and there, over that water, she pronounced a dreadful curse on the conjuror's head with the words:

> *May he wander endlessly,*
> *At every step, a stumbling.*
> *At every stumbling, a fall.*
> *At every fall, a broken bone,*

> *Not of the largest, nor of the least,*
> *But the bones of his neck, every time.*

Some ways off, walking across his farm back to his home, Goronwy felt the curse take root, for he was well-taught in the ways of old craft, and he could feel the sensation of the curse laid upon his bones, heavy and dark. But even this witchery was no match for the conjuror, for he knew just what to do. He went off into the trees, and he searched for that mushroom called *witch's butter*, and with certain words of old craft, he began placing pins into the mushroom slowly, one after another.

It was not long before old Bella Fawr came before him, shrieking and contorted in pain, still limping from the wound of the silver coin, begging him to take the pins out and cease her torment. But Goronwy Tudor only raised one eyebrow then, and told her that he would kill her and all who follow her unless she said the exact words to undo the curse she had placed upon him, which were:

> *God's blessing be upon thee*
> *And everything that thou possessest*

And such was her agony that the witch agreed readily, and the conjuror being a man of his word, he removed the pins, and allowed the greatest of the Llanddona witches to leave with her life.

What the witch did not know, however, was that from the very moment she pronounced those words, Goronwy Tudor's land became immune to all of the sorceries of her people for all time, and none of his crops, nor his livestock, nor his family, nor his descendants could ever be harmed by their witchcraft again.

Through Thick and Thin
New World

No one knew where Phoebe Ward came from, who her people were, or why she had settled in Northampton County, North Carolina. What was certain to all local residents was that old Phoebe was a witch. And she earned her living as many other witches did in ages past: by demanding the hospitality and generosity of neighbors, who were sure to oblige, lest they risk incurring the witch's curse upon the entire household.

It was said that old Phoebe could, by her black art, transform anyone she wished into a horse, and ride them through the fields until daybreak, at which point the victim would wake up exhausted and sore, having no idea what had transpired during the night. Steeds under her control could be commanded to leap across a river if the witch desired, and to travel faster than any normal horse ever could. "Through thick, and through thin," she would say, and off her steed would gallop, to travel any distance to her desired location. Such was the extent of Phoebe Ward's craft.

Nor were local residents safe inside their homes at night, for old Phoebe could change herself into a whisp of smoke in order to travel through keyholes, entering any house of her choosing. But none of these trappings were necessary for her nocturnal revels, for the witch also possessed a special, magical grease, an ointment that, when rubbed on her skin, allowed her to slip out of her own flesh and bones and fly through the air, then return when her mischief was done.

Though by most accounts, the locals feared old Phoebe and gave her whatever she demanded when visiting their home, there were occasions when her demands perhaps went too far at the abuse of her hosts. To appease the witch with a bit of butter or cornmeal is one thing, but to be forced to house her indefinitely is quite another. Thus, people forced to take in old Phoebe resorted to a few tricks in order to get her to leave without confronting her directly.

One trick involved throwing dried red pepper into an open fire, the smoke of which she could not stand, causing her to depart at once. Another involved the use of pins placed in chairs so that when the witch took a seat, she received a sharp prick quite by surprise. These ruses caused old Phoebe great annoyance, of course, but no lasting harm. Eventually, she became quite wise to them, refusing to sit in the chair with the pin hidden in its cushion, or even refusing to visit the home where such traps were already set for her, passing it by on the road with no other reason or explanation than her keen witch-sense.

But country witches, unlike town witches, are quite long-lived, for in such remote places, where doctors were few and far between in ages past, their knowledge of the healing arts rendered them invaluable. Old Phoebe Ward may have suffered the odd prank or trick at her expense, but by no account did she ever face the hangman's noose for her witchcraft, living to quite an impossibly old age. And as very old witches often do, it is most likely that she imparted her craft to one or more persons desirous of such power, and so her witchcraft may yet live on, they say.

The Spelled Left Eye
Cornwall

It was a great many generations ago, on Hallan Eve, that a housekeeper by the name of An' Pee Tregeer embarked upon the road. On this night, of all the nights of the year, one is more likely to encounter spirits or stumble upon the hidden workings of witches. Nonetheless, the woman desired to go to market before the coming of dark in order to purchase a few small things for herself, and so she set off to the home of a friend who might accompany her to town.

Now, this friend, whose name was Jenny Trayer, earned much of her living as a white witch or charmer, helping folks find lost items, protect themselves against enemies, or ensure the prosperity of their farm—all for the right price, of course. There were even some who whispered that the Trayers both, man and wife, were in league with the Old One and practiced a darker craft, for Tom Trayer always had good fortune at sea when others had none, with a favorable wind always in his sails and fish eager to jump into his nets, even when poorer fortunes were had by all around him.

As An' Pee arrived at the home of the Trayer couple, she found the front door quite shut, which was unusual, for their custom was to leave it open for all to enter as they pleased. She could hear voices conversing inside with quite a serious tone, and so she succumbed to curiosity and peeked through the latch-hole, which is just the size of one's finger.

The inside was quite dark; only a single candle illuminated the space, but she could just make out her friend Jenny standing before her husband. She was holding a limpet shell, which is shaped like a shallow bowl, and from its basin, drawing away on her finger some manner of ointment or grease, which she then smeared on the eyes of the man, muttering something quietly as she did so.

An' Pee knocked on the door then, and she watched as Jenny hid the limpet shell away in a cabinet and wiped her hands before answering the door. She was welcomed in as usual and offered drink and a bit of cake. Jenny's husband was less welcoming, though, and scowled at the visitor the entire time, evidently annoyed by the interruption.

"Let me go and fetch the cake," said Jenny.

"I'll fetch the drink, I suppose," said her husband, reluctantly.

As soon as they left the room, of course, curious An' Pee made her way to the cabinet where the limpet shell was hidden, and took a bit of its ointment on her own finger. She dabbed it on her left eye, but before she had time to anoint the other, she heard the couple returning, and she quickly returned the shell to its hiding place and sat down, folding her hands in her lap as before.

Jenny declined to go with An' Pee to town, though, for she had matters to attend to on her own, or so she said. And so An' Pee continued down the road a ways on foot, until at last, she came to the town market just as the sun began to set in the distance. Realizing that it was quite later in the evening than she had hoped for, she made quick work of her errands, darting here and there in order to make her purchases speedily, for all manner of things wander about on such a dark night as Hallan Eve, and she was eager to return home.

As she was gathering up her parcels to leave, she spied her friend's husband, the Trayer man, whom she had seen not an hour before, wandering among the stalls of the market. He was eagerly snatching this and that as he pleased, taking a length of cloth from this table, and a bottle of whisky from that one, until at last his arms were full. None seemed to notice him as he went, which was strange, but An' Pee decided at last to intervene.

"Tom Trayer," she said sternly, standing before him, "put those parcels down this instant unless you intend on paying these good people."

The man looked shocked, and his face went pale for a moment. "From which eye can you see me, woman?" he said with a snarl.

An' Pee was confused by the question, but she blinked her right eye, and then her left eye, and wouldn't you know that the man disappeared when her left one was closed. "I see you with my left eye, Tom," she said.

"Then that left eye shall serve you no more, you meddlesome thing." And with that, he blew into her left eye, and disappeared before her, his laughter echoing all around her.

The woman felt a terrible pain then, as if her left eye had been stabbed with a needle. Her sight in that eye went black, and she was doubled over in agony. Though most of the market stalls were closing, and the merchants packing away to leave for the night, one woman was kind enough to offer her a cloth and some water to clean her ailing eye, which helped with the pain, and though her vision was blurry, she was able to see with it, after a fashion, and was able to continue home.

Fearing that Tom Trayer was still hounding her steps, she made her way quickly, but it had grown quite dark, and her vision proved increasingly poor. The road seemed to shift and move before her, and a stone that appeared to be on her left would the next moment be on her right, until she at last realized that she had lost her way in the darkness and had mistakenly stumbled onto a path that looked strange to her.

Seeing faint lights in the distance, An' Pee wandered towards them, hoping for a safe place to rest, but when she saw the gathering she had come upon at last, she hid behind a stone out of fear. There, gathered in a great mass, was a crowd of people who were very strange in appearance. Their faces and the proportions of their bodies were all wrong, such that she could tell they were not people at all, but something only somewhat like them. They seemed to be holding a festival of some kind, and dancing, and playing games, drinking and singing, but their appearance was frightening to her, and she felt deep in her bones and in her blood that she was not meant to be witnessing the sight before her, that she had somehow trespassed upon a gathering not meant for human eyes.

Try to hide as she might, it was not long, of course, before she was found out and spied by one of the strange company, who screamed to the others, and they seized her then with many hands, and climbed upon her back to hold her down, and pulled at her hair and face, tormenting her, and An' Pee felt her heart pounding in her chest so hard with fear that she was sure she would die of fright.

When she awoke by the side of the road, the woman thought for a moment that it had been some sort of dream or sickness caused by the witch-man's blast, but her clothes were torn by the many hands that were upon her. When she looked around her, she realized, of course, where she was. In her blindness and delirium, she had wandered onto that haunted stretch called the Gump, where Carn Kenidjack still stands, a hill with ancient stones laid by pre-Christian tribes long dead, where ghosts, faeries, and other dark spirits are said to hold their revels under the veil of night. She knew then the truth of such tales, for she had seen the spirits there with her own left eye, and she had lived to see the morning, though none would believe her story for the rest of her days.

The Broom-Wives
Scotland

In another age, the old farmland of Delnabo was split between three tenant farming families, and one of these estates was farmed by a poor man and wife. Although the neighboring farms fared quite well, wanting for nothing, their own farm produced little. This was odd, considering the fact that the same seasons fell on their farm as fell on the others; the same rains and frosts, the same unruly summers and unpredictable springs. Their neighbors made such a sound living that their kitchens were ever stocked, and their worries few, while the poor man and wife feared always for their uncertain future.

One day, the wives of the three farms were gathered together to wash their clothes in the waters of the River Avon, at a place where the currents slowed into a wide and tranquil pool. They were chatting leisurely about this and that, as was their custom, when the two wives of the prosperous farms felt pity for the third wife. They had watched her warm and sunny disposition wither over the last year and grow cold and distant, and they knew that times for the woman and her husband must be hard indeed.

"What would you give," asked one of the other wives, "to be safe from hunger and poverty, to be assured of good harvests for the rest of your life?"

The poor woman thought it a very strange question. "I would give anything, I should think," she answered. "If such things were possible."

The two other wives gave one another a sly look then, as if smiling at some secret shared between them. "Perhaps she would, then," said one of the wives.

"Perhaps she could, then," said the other, quite mysteriously, rubbing her chin and looking the poor farmer's wife up and down, as if studying her. "Very well," she said at last. "Come you at midnight to meet us here, at this very spot, and wear a pretty dress, and tell not your husband."

The poor wife looked puzzled. "But surely he will know I have left our bed and wandered out at night."

At this, the two other wives shared a hearty laugh. "Take you that old broom from beside your hearth, and place it in bed next to your husband, and he shall be none the wiser. We've employed this trick for many years, and neither of our husbands can tell the difference."

The poor wife laughed as well, and she agreed to do as she was instructed, for she was eager to know what secret the two other wives kept between them that made them so sure of their farms' prosperity. As she went home with their laundry that day, she was bristling with anticipation and excitement at what might be their farm's salvation.

But as the house of the afternoon passed, she grew quite suspicious. Why was she asked to wear a pretty dress? And what could or would she be expected to do? And why, if their secret was such a blessing, should she be asked to keep it secret? At last, she decided to tell her husband, for they shared a true love between them, and they had always made all of their decisions together as one.

And when she told him about their conversation down by the water and how sure the other wives were of their farms' harvests, he was as puzzled as she. Their fear, of course, was that something nefarious would be expected of her in exchange for the farm's success, a prospect they both found disturbing. They sat about their fire that evening, drinking and smoking and talking, and at last, they came up with a plan together. The husband would go in the wife's stead, wearing her pretty dress and a cloth about his head to make him look like a woman, which would surely be a sufficient disguise in the dark.

As the farmer made his way over the hills toward the water, he thought he saw strange lights in the distance, and then heard much shouting and laughing, as if a great party were going on. It was near midnight, and the wind was cold, and his wife's pretty dress did little to warm him, but he pressed on. He had come this far, after all. And he was desirous to know the secret of the farmers' wives.

There, all about the water's edge, was a great gathering of witches—not only the two women, but women and men of every age and ilk, all gathered together in the dark, with only a few torches to light the scene. Some paddled in riddles—a type of large sieve—using their brooms as oars, holding fir torches strangely in their left hands. Some sailed across the air on forked branches; others rode pigs and goats and all manner of creatures. Some swam in the dark water, singing and laughing together as if they were quite drunk. And in the middle of this gathering, there in the deepest part of the water, stood an immense figure with the head of a horned beast, gazing pridefully upon this throng of witches, who circled him, celebrating and making all sorts of merriment.

It was then that the farmer was taken by surprise, for the two other wives had spotted him, and they joined him on either side, taking his two arms in their own as if to lead him forward towards some uncertain fate.

"What a pretty dress you have," said one of the witches. "You make a lovely bride, indeed."

"And a lovely sister, after tonight," said the other witch. "For once the Old One accepts your hand, we will be as family, and you need have no fear of bad harvests."

The two witches explained to him what was to follow, that they would approach on their sieves in order to announce to their Devil the arrival of a new bride, and then they would return to collect her. Neither suspected, of course, that this was the husband in disguise; they were utterly fooled, which was quite lucky for the farmer, for terrible things are known to happen to those who wander upon a gathering of witches uninvited.

As the witches climbed into their sieves, holding up their fir torches and making their way to the Old One, the farmer called out after them, "Godspeed, ladies!" at which the magic suspending them on the water's surface was broken, and all of the witch-vessels fell into the water, leaving them flailing and splashing about, their fir torches extinguished. Those in the air riding forked branches and brooms and goats all fell instantly, some landing on top of others with a scream. The witches all ran off in different directions, taking a variety of forms as they did so. Some became hares, and others became cats, or birds, or black dogs, all scampering away from sight.

The Devil gave a great bellow then, a terrible moaning roar the likes of which the man never heard, and an awful fear took root in him, for all of the torches had gone out now and he was there in the utter darkness, all alone with the Devil himself. And so he fled as fast as his legs could carry him, his dress disheveled in the wind and falling off one shoulder as he made his way home.

When he arrived at the little farmhouse, he told his wife all that had happened, much to her disbelief, and they sat up all night long until dawn, for they were greatly afraid that the Devil or the witches would visit vengeance upon them. After the sun rose, it was not the Devil, but the husbands of the other two wives who knocked upon their door, for they had heard the screaming and shouting of the night before nearby at the water's edge, and they wanted to know if the couple had seen anything strange.

"Perhaps you should ask your wives," said the farmer's wife.

"I would," replied the one farmer, "but she was sleeping so soundly when I left, her thick hair on the pillow and the tip of one toe sticking out from under the blanket."

"Mine as well," added the second farmer. "She sleeps so deeply and so still, one might mistake her for a length of wood."

The Drowned Suitors
Isle of Man

It is said that, in ancient times, there lived a powerful witch on the Isle of Man by the name of Tehi-Tegi. Though cruel of heart and full of malice, she was beautiful to behold, they say, and there was no lovelier creature than her on the entire island in her day. But this was not all, for the witch had mastered the arts of fascination and love-spelling, and by her craft, she lured men away from all they held dear.

Those men unlucky enough to be ensnared by the sorceries of Tehi-Tegi left behind their homes and their wives. They abandoned their fields to ruin and their livestock to starvation. Their houses became overgrown with weeds and vines, and their farms fell into disarray. They wandered, disheveled, their clothes in tatters, giving up even the will to clean and feed themselves, all for want of following the witch wherever she would go.

And at last, it came to be that all of the men of the island were ensorcelled by the witch and followed her wherever she went in a great mass of entranced suitors, longing even for the sight of her beautiful face or the sound of her soft voice, all imagining that she loved them and that they would one day perhaps become her husband.

This, however, was not her design. One day, when she had enraptured the last of the men of the island, she climbed upon her white horse, which was a regal, graceful creature befitting her own beauty, and announced that she would ride through each of the provinces of that land. She bade her spell-bound horde of men to follow her, and they did so, wandering from town to town, which was surely a wild and strange sight to behold.

Finally, she came to a deep river, and though her many men adored her, they were afraid to cross it on foot, for it was dangerous even in the best weather. She assured them of their safety then, and she used her powers of witchery to calm the waters and the wind so that they could cross it. Eagerly, they followed her then, but as soon as Tehi-Tegi had made her way across almost to the other shore, she transformed herself into a wren and flew off above, and her white horse became a fish and swam away below, and then the waters rushed in, and the wind rose in a great swell, and the river raged over the entire company, drowning most of the men behind her.

And it is said that this is the reason the wren is hunted on the Isle of Man on St. Stephen's Day, for the witch Tehi-Tegi may still roam the island in that form, watching and listening from the branches of trees, waiting for the day this tale might be forgotten so that she might ride her pale horse about once more in her old human form, ensnaring the men of the island again with her beauty and her magic, and leading them all to a terrible death by drowning.

The Seventh Witch
New World

Once, long ago, along the winding path of the Cheat River in West Virginia, there lived a portly old man who was called Old Braham. He had restored an old cabin there overlooking the river over the course of a summer, and though folks warned him that the property was strange and haunted, he would hear none of it, and made of it a pleasant and comfortable home where he might set up a small farm. He worked diligently to restore the place, and in the end, the only reminder of what it was before was an old picture of a woman hung upon the wall, which he decided to keep.

It was not long after he was settled that strange things began happening in that place. He would hear sounds at night near the hearth, much like voices, and he would rise from his bed and run through the cabin with his gun to find the intruders, but there would be no one there, only a strong rush of wind going up the chimney, which was always cold.

One night, he decided to take a different approach. He stayed perfectly still in his bed, pretending to sleep, until the voices began, and then he proceeded only to listen, not making a sound so as not to disturb them. He could make out the voices of six different men, all gathered around his hearth, whispering.

"This place was our own long before it was his," said the first.

"Remove the hearthstone, and take out the grease," said the second.

"And behind it, the bridles as well," said the third.

"We'll anoint ourselves thrice with our witch's grease, on brow and throat and chest," said the fourth.

"And up the chimney we'll fly, to ride the wind across these hills," said the fifth.

"And we'll bridle what man or beast we will, and ride them the rest of the way, to the meeting of the witches on the old mountaintop," said the sixth.

At hearing all of this, Old Braham was filled with fear, for he knew that witching folk were a dangerous matter indeed, and he realized that he had set up his home in an old witch-house, the sort of abandoned ruin that witches prefer to use for their strange business.

"But wait," interrupted the first witch-man. "Where is the seventh of our number?"

"No matter," said another, "for there are seven calves in yonder field, leaving one behind for the seventh among us."

And with that, the witch-men each anointed themselves with the charmed grease, and Old Braham could hear the same cold wind rush up the chimney again as he had all those nights before, and the witch-men were whisked away through the hearth with their magic bridles. He watched through his window as they landed in the nearby field, placing their bridles in the mouths of six of his young calves, then mounting them and riding them off into the night, towards a great, dark mountain that stood in the distance.

But Old Braham felt afraid no longer, and he decided at that moment that he would become a witch-man himself. If that was what it took to find and punish the lot of them and chase them away from his home, then so be it. And so he anointed himself with the witch-grease thrice, upon his brow and throat and chest, and holding the last bridle in his hands, he was whisked up the chimney into the black night, landing softly in the nearby field.

Now, the witch-men had taken the strongest-looking calves, but they had left the little black one behind. And Old Braham smiled at this, for although the remaining calf was the smallest, it was also the fastest. He slid the bridle gently into its mouth, then mounted it, and the little black calf began walking upon the very air, rising up through the wind, and making its way toward the towering mountain in the distance.

Its pace quickened as they went, and before long, Old Braham could see the six witch-men ahead of him, and he darted past each, kicking them as he went, so that they flew off their calves and fell into the thick woods below with a scream. But just after he kicked the last witch-man off of his calf, he was caught on a very tall tree and knocked from his own witch-steed, falling and falling until he landed on the ground, his calf trotting away from him in the distance.

Relieved to find himself uninjured, he decided to walk home, but it was then that a great black cat leapt onto his back from a nearby tree, scratching and clawing him badly, and the thing was nearly as big as Braham himself, and he could not shake it off nor overpower it. At last, the enormous black cat slid a bridle into Braham's own mouth.

"See now, foolish man!" cried the black cat with great glowing eyes. "You thought you'd ride your way to the witches' meeting? And so you shall." And then the black cat uncurled its back, and its spine lengthened, and it became an old woman, laughing at him.

Braham tried to yell out for help, but he could not. He tried to fight and resist, but he could not. The magic bridle held him fast, such that he was now enslaved to serve the witch, no matter what was asked of him.

"And now I," said the old woman, "the seventh of the Cheat River Witches, shall ride on your tired back, all the way to the mountaintop." And with that, she mounted him, and they made their way up and up, weaving between trees and over rocks, until they came to the meeting place of the witches high upon the mountain.

Old Braham was tied to a nearby tree, and though he could not make out what went on during the meeting, he heard a great many voices, some familiar to him and some unfamiliar, and he saw strange lights and heard strange music and laughter and dancing, and when at last the old witch returned to ride home, she was quite drunk and depleted, and she decided then to lay down nearby and take a bit of rest before returning down the mountain again.

It was then that Braham seized his moment of opportunity, carefully and quietly slipping the bit and bridle from his own mouth, and placing it deftly upon the witch so as not to wake her. When he climbed onto her back, she tried to let out a scream, for Old Braham was quite a large man, but the scream stuck in her throat, and she could do naught but obey his will as long as the bridle was in place.

"I carried you all the way up the mountain," boomed Old Braham. "Surely, it's only fair you should carry me back down again."

And so he rode the witch all the way back down, nor was he gentle as he did so, for he made sure to hit the occasional rock or tree branch, just for his own amusement. And when at last they glided down into the field behind his cabin, the witch was utterly spent, and she cried out in agony that she could take no more, begging for mercy.

Old Braham felt pity for her then, and he climbed off her back, walking beside her the rest of the way to his cabin, though he did not remove the bridle, lest she turn on him with all of her powers. He was, after all, quite new to witchcraft, and surely the old witch could take his life in but a moment if she were freed. She slumped and pouted, but walked peacefully beside him the rest of the way, and when he opened the cabin door, she made her way inside, walking over to the old fireplace, and taking from behind another loose stone a small cooking pan.

The old woman tried to say something, but because of the bridle, it came out only as a mumble. She fell to the floor in tears, for she felt quite humiliated in that moment. Succumbing to a wave of pity, Braham reached out to her and removed the bridle.

"This was my own home once, you know," she said sadly, cradling the little metal pan she had retrieved from behind the fireplace stone. And Braham thought to himself that perhaps her punishment had been sufficient, and they might come to some kind of peace between them.

"Now, do not move," said Old Braham, "for I've a silver bullet and a gun beside my bed. I'm going to grab them now for my own safety, and if you've moved when I return, I'll end you as sure as anything."

The old woman agreed, but as Braham left the room, she began polishing and polishing the little pan, gazing into its reflective surface and rocking back and forth, for in this way the old witches of that area would work their darkest craft. And she tapped her ring upon it three times, and she called out into the reflection in its surface at last:

> *I pledge anew my very soul to the Devil*
> *And consecrate myself to his designs,*
> *On condition that Old Ebenezer Braham*
> *Shall die as surely as the sun does rise.*

But before she could finish working the charm, Old Braham fired that silver bullet. There was no time to aim at the witch, of course, so he aimed at the old picture that hung on the wall, for he knew now that was her likeness. At that very moment, the witch screamed out in pain and fell dead upon the floor, as surely as if the bullet had gone through her very own heart.

What became of Old Braham after that night is uncertain. Some believe he made his own deal with the Devil and continues his witching ways to this very day. Others believe he became a good witch-man, a healer and herb doctor, the kind who helped neighbors when doctors were few in those mountains. But for many years after, folks along Cheat River would say that a little black calf could be seen floating above the line of trees, making its way up the mountain, and if the moon was bright enough, one could just make out a mysterious rider upon its back.

Nine Witch-Knots
Scotland

There lived once, in a time long ago, back in the age of castles and kings, a young couple very much in love. Now, the young man's mother was opposed to their marriage, and vehemently so, whether due to the young woman's family, or her looks, or some facet of her character. None could say for certain the reason, for the young man's mother was possessed of a hateful nature, and her moods came without cause or warning. Worse still, the woman was a well-known witch, a fact that was not lost on the young man, who loved his sweetheart dearly and did not want any harm to come to her.

Eventually, though, the two were wed and made their home together, and though Willie—for that was the young man's name—lived in fear of his mother's retribution, his wife seemed little bothered. And so they were happy together as man and wife, and soon the woman was pregnant with their child, and the two were made happier still, full of hope and expectation for their new family, and they had all but forgotten about the man's witch-mother and her hatred for their union.

Their happiness did not last, however. For nine months went by, and then many days after, and many more after that, and still, the bairn did not come. To the torment of the mother, the thing refused to be born, and she grew pale and weak, gaunt and frail, even as the midwives scurried about her day after day, trying every craft known to them, all to no avail, until at last she could no longer walk and lay at all hours in her sickbed, tortured and miserable. The healers at last said that the woman would die in a matter of days, and the infant with her.

And so Willie went to his mother's house, for he suspected this was all the work of his mother's witchcraft. He begged with her, pleading that she should remove the charm she had placed upon his wife so that the bairn might come at last. "Please," said Willie to his witch-mother, "undo this witchery. My love has gold and silver, and fine steeds, and her family has much land, and any of this can be yours if only you will remove the curse."

But Willie's mother was unmoved. "I care not for her gold or silver or horses or land, boy," said the witch. "I told you not to marry her, and you defied me. So she will die, and when she and the bairn are both cold and dead and rotten in the ground, you shall marry another, as you should have done in the first place."

"I'll marry no other," said Willie. And with that, he left his mother's house, and could find no comfort in anything, for he knew then that his wife and child were both cursed to die, and that no manner of pleading could move his own mother to remove the terrible curse.

But that night, as he slept, Willie was visited by a strange spirit, and this spirit told him of a way to undo the witch's curse, that he must go out to the marketplace and purchase a loaf of wax, then shape it in the form of a babe, and swaddle it with cloth just like it was his own. Then, he was to invite his witch-mother to the child's christening, where he would have them pretend to christen the wax bairn as he listened to the words his mother would say. The spirit assured him that only hearing these words would set free his wife and child.

And so, as instructed, Willie fashioned the wax babe and orchestrated its christening, and he invited his mother to attend. He waited out of sight in order to watch and listen to what she said as she entered. And when his mother came into the church and saw what looked like a child about to be christened, she flew into a rage.

"Who did this?" she cried out, her eyes wild with hatred. "Who loosened my nine witch-knots? Who removed the woodbine hung in her bower? Who took the black charm I set beneath her bed?"

As hastily as his legs could carry him, Willie ran then to his love's chambers and began searching wildly about the room. He found the length of nine witch-knots, and untied them. He found the woodbine, and cast it into the fire. He found the charm beneath the bed, and threw it into a nearby stream to be carried far away. And at this, the child came quickly, and without too much difficulty, and his wife's health was restored.

Whatever became of Willie's witch-mother, however, we cannot say for certain. Perhaps, learning that her witchcraft had been undone by the instructions of a spirit, she was humbled after that, and they were able to get on somewhat better than before. For when spirits intervene, it is usually best to set a new course and move on.

The Horned Women
Ireland

A very long time ago, there lived a wealthy woman who had a splendid home and many healthy children, and there was little in the world that is good of which she did not have her own fair share. She had many servants, and the security of gold, and a prosperous farm. But a life of luxury can often breed discontentment.

With all of her servants overburdened with work, the woman sat up late one night by the fire, carding wool, and she wished to herself that some other would come and take on the task. Why, after all, should a woman of means be set to carding her own wool? And it was then, as soon as the wish was spoken aloud to herself, that there came a knock at the door of the house.

There, in the foot of her doorway, stood a woman with a great horn growing from her own forehead. "I am the Witch of One Horn," said the figure, "and your home be open unto me." The woman found herself unable to resist the witch's words, and so she allowed her in. The witch seated herself and began carding wool with great speed and intensity then, and after a while, she spoke. "Where are my sisters? The hour grows late."

It was then that another knocked upon the door. It was yet another witch like the first, but this one had two horns growing from her head and a spinning wheel under her arm. "I am the Witch of Two Horns," said the figure, "and your home be open unto me." Like before, the woman found herself unable to resist the witch's strange powers, and so she allowed her in. As soon as the witch seated herself beside the fire, she began to spin wool with great alacrity.

And this procession went on quite late into the night and early morning: more and more witches arrived at the door, and the wealthy woman became their captive host, unable to move or speak to resist the compelling power of their witchcraft, until at last there were twelve horned women all seated together, working the wool, talking and laughing. The last of their number was a frightening figure, for the twelve horns upon her head were all clustered together so that they resembled a twisted crown.

Once the women had finished with the wool, they moved on to other business of witchery. They compelled the woman's husband and children to a death-like sleep, and took some of their blood, and baked it into cakes, of which they ate some. They charmed the door of the house to always allow them entry, that they might never be refused. They ensorcelled all of the wool they had spun that it might tie them to that place forever, and that the woman's home and all that she possessed should be theirs from that day until Doomsday.

Having done all of this, the witches took to amusing themselves with the woman's suffering. They tasked her with a series of impossible things, which the woman was compelled by their magic to do, but could never complete.

"Churn for us some butter," said the Witch of Three Horns, "using your feet instead of your hands." And the woman could not resist their craft, and she was forced to churn butter by gripping the churn between the soles of her feet. And the witches laughed.

"Chop for us some wood," said the Witch of Nine Horns, "using only a spoon." And the woman could not resist their craft, and she was forced to hack away at a tree using only a blunt spoon. And the witches cackled in even greater amusement.

"I've got one," said the Witch of Twelve Horns, who could hardly speak through her laughter. "Bring us some water from the well...with this..." And the witch handed the woman a sieve, and all twelve of the witches fell into riotous laughter, rolling around on the floor.

The woman again could not resist their sorcery, and so she was forced to walk down to the well, and to dip the sieve into the water again and again, but of course no water could it hold. As she wept into the well, terrified of what new horror would befall her family, her teardrops fell onto the black surface of the water, and a voice arose from its depths.

"Fear not, child," said the Spirit in the Well. "Put down the sieve, and cease this business."

The woman was quite startled, but found that she was able to put down the sieve and stop the pointless task at last. "Are you yet another witch, Spirit? Won't you have mercy on me and my family?"

"I am older than those that torment you," said the Spirit in the Well, "and I know well their ways."

"Won't you help us, then?" the woman begged.

"None can help you," the voice replied. "None can save you. But if you heed my words, I will teach you some manner of craft of your own, and you may yet save yourself." And then the Spirit in the Well imparted to her a series of instructions she was to carry out perfectly, and the woman set to her tasks, for it was the only way to save her family.

First, she yelled at the top of her lungs, "The mountain of the twelve women is burning!" At this, all twelve witches fled shrieking into the darkness towards a towering mountain in the distance, thinking that their ancient home was in danger. And this bought the woman time to work her own witchery against them.

Next, in their absence, the woman gathered up the bowl of water that had been used to wash her children's feet earlier that evening, and she sprinkled it upon the doorway, muttering charms taught to her by the Spirit in the Well.

Then she took some of the cakes the witches had baked with the blood of her husband and children in them, and she gave each of them a piece of it to eat, and they were restored from their death-like sleep.

Lastly, she took a portion of the wool the witches had spun, and she stuck it in a padlocked chest so that it hung half-in and half-out, pinched by the tightly locked lid.

When the witches returned, they were furious, having realized of course that it was all a trick, and that their mountain was in fact not burning at all. They screamed that they would have terrible vengeance upon the woman, their eyes wide with blind rage, but they found the door locked and could not open it.

"I call upon the charmed beams of this doorway," said the Witch of Three Horns, gravely. "Open, and allow us entry."

"I cannot," replied the doorway, "for I am yours no longer. Another has bathed me with the water of her children's feet."

"I call upon those ensnared by our blood-cakes," said the Witch of Nine Horns, her voice seething with venom. "Rise up, and open this door that we might enter."

"We will not," replied the woman's children and husband, "for our blood is our own again, and your cake-charm is undone."

"I call upon the wool we spelled this night," said the Witch of Twelve Horns, her great voice booming with wrath. "Undo this white witch's charm-work, that we might enter this house and taste her blood."

"I cannot," replied the wool, "for I am pinched and strained, and I cannot resist the true mistress of this house."

And at last, having exhausted all of their charms, the witches were forced to leave, and they flew through the air, screaming insults and vile things at the woman, who had outsmarted them. And one of them dropped the mantle that she wore about her shoulders as she left, and it fell upon the ground, and the family gathered it up the next day, and they kept it as a reminder of that terrible night. The mantle hung over the fireplace for many generations in that family, who did, over time, learn some manner of craft of their own in order to protect themselves from malevolent witches. And for all we know, the mantle may still hang in that home today.

The Witch's Bit
New World

They say that once, many generations ago, there lived out in the wilds of Canada an old charm-worker, healer, and witch-doctor, whose specialty was helping those suffering from witch-riding, which is a specific form of torment by means of witchcraft.

While many witches know how to cast a curse or steal the goodness of one's land, certain witches are said to be able to sneak into one's room at night, and by secret charms, turn a person into a steed, riding them around all night long so that they wake up worse for wear, and often eventually grow quite ill and weak.

One day, there came a man to the witch-doctor's door who claimed to be suffering from this very ailment. The man was disheveled and haggard, and appeared to be suffering a great deal. "Tell me," said the old witch-doctor, "who is the witch you suspect of riding you at night?"

The man looked confused. "It is not one witch who rides me, but a whole congregation of them, one after the other. And I have no power to resist, like a horse in a bridle. I have walked fifty long miles to come to see you, and even that distance is as nothing compared to the running I am forced to do each night."

The witch-doctor was baffled by this, quite naturally, for fifty miles is a very long ways to walk. But when he asked the poor man to open his mouth, he saw for himself that his account was true, for there along the corners of his mouth were deep sores, just where the edges of a hard metal bit would rest in a horse's mouth.

The Blighted Orchard
England

It happened once in the county of Gloucestershire that a traveler, who was quite poor and seeking farm work, came upon a great orchard in the countryside. Though the land around was lush and green, every tree on that orchard was twisted, dry, and barren.

The traveler approached the owner of the farm, who was walking among the dead orchard, weeping and wringing his hands. "What sort of blight is this," he asked, "that has ravaged only your own orchard, and not those of your neighbors? Every other fruiting tree for miles is heavy with harvest."

"It is no ordinary blight," replied the man in tears, "but the curse of a dark wizard who lives nearby."

"Surely you do not truly believe in such nonsense," said the traveler.

"You should not speak so," he replied, eyes wide with fear. The man looked about him then carefully, as if he were afraid of being watched and overheard by someone.

"And why not? Only children believe in such foolishness. What grown man fears witches and wizards and their curses?"

At that moment, a single branch of one of the blackened trees cracked and fell, landing just between the two, giving the both of them a great shock. A flock of crows fluttered, lifting all together from their perches in the tree, cackling as they went.

"You should not speak so, sir," continued the owner of the cursed orchard, "for you know not what harm may come to you. The witches of this area have amassed great power, and that is all I will say on the matter, for it is unwise to speak of the witching folk any more than necessary."

The traveler felt a cold wind blow through him. Above him, on a single skeletal branch, one crow remained, tilting its head and peering at him with its glossy black eye.

"You know for a fact that a curse was laid here?"

"I do, sir. I shouldn't be telling you this, but for your own safety, you must understand. The old witch-man paid a visit to the house some months ago, and having been refused hospitality, left on his way. But before he did, I saw myself how he placed one hand on a single tree and began speaking to it, muttering words I could not make out, as if to charm the very life from the branches. Shortly after, all of the fruit began to spoil, and one tree after another died, even while every other orchard in the county did prosper."

Above their heads, the single remaining crow cried out sharply, then flew off with great haste, as if to some appointed task. The man went pale and put his hand over his mouth. "Go now," he said to the traveler at last, "and do not return to this place. Remember what I have told you, but speak of it not."

Most wisely, the traveler left then, and went on his way, speaking not to another soul until he reached the next county. He never found out what became of the farmer who spoke of the witches that day. He seldom spoke of that day himself, and on the rare occasion when he did, he was sure to do so only indoors, with every window shut tight—so that his tale would not be overheard by the many ears of the witching folk, who may yet be listening.

The Burning Peat
Scotland

In ages past, it was a long-held superstition in Scotland never to share one's fire with another household on New Year's Day, nor on any of the quarter days (these days being Candlemas, Beltane, Lammas, and Hallowmas). Such fires were empowered with protective qualities for keeping the wicked at bay, and to allow a neighbor to take burning peat from one's home would subvert the warding, leaving the gates open to mischief at the hands of all manner of spirits and witches.

Once, on a New Year's Day a very long time ago, a little old woman came to a local weaver's house, begging for a bit of burning peat. "Be it any day, I have need, good woman," she said pleadingly. "Please be kind enough to share your fire with me. I've been hungry and cold two days now."

The weaver woman, being kind-hearted, did as she asked, but as soon as her visitor made her way home with her smoldering bucket in hand, odd things began happening in the house. The fireplace hooks would swing back and forth of their own volition. Strange shadows could be seen about the cottage at night. Worst of all, the cows refused to give milk.

After several days, the weaver woman consulted a local skilly man for advice, for he knew of such things, having some knowledge of the forbidden arts himself. "Take a bit of burning peat," the skilly man said, "and cast it into a tub of cold water. It is by your fire that the witch torments you, and it is by cold water that her craft may be drowned."

And so the weaver woman did as the skilly man advised her, taking a bit of smoldering peat from her own fireplace, and casting it into a tub filled with cold water. However, the charm was not complete, for the thing had split in two on the edge of the tub, half falling into the water, and half falling on the floor. Immediately, she heard a knocking at the door. It was the little old woman from a few days before, the one with whom she had shared her fire in a moment of pity.

"Please, good woman, may I replenish my fire from your own? I am so cold and wet from the rain."

"It has not rained this day, as well you know," said the weaver woman.

Seeing that she had been caught in a lie, the woman's face changed then, and all sweetness left her voice. "Then give it to me regardless, fool, or I'll torment you until your dying day," spat the witch.

"We'll see about that," said the weaver woman, who then promptly slammed the door and gathered up the other half of the smoldering peat with a shovel, casting it into the tub. It sizzled and hissed with steam.

When she returned to her front door, her visitor had completely vanished, as if into the very air. She found the tub, which she expected to be filthy with ash, to be perfectly clean already. What's more, it was full to the brim with freshly churned butter. Her cows began to give milk again soon afterwards, and the weaver woman never again gave away her fire on New Year's Day.

The Nail-Stuck Heart
Wales

To refuse a beggar was, in the old times, a grave matter indeed, for such was the outward appearance of many witching folk. Much like faeries—for witches of the old stories are part-human and part-other—they were capable of terrible revenge upon the selfish and the callous. Often, the only true remedy was to instigate a repetition of the request, so that one might behave correctly the second time.

It happened long ago that a farmer's wife was visited by an old beggar woman, who asked only for a potato or two so that she might eat that day. The woman of the house refused, turning her away empty-handed, even though she herself had plenty to share and it would have been as nothing to offer her a few potatoes from her cellar.

And so the beggar went on her way, but as she did so, she picked up a bit of hay from the ground, muttering under her breath something that sounded like gibberish, perhaps mixed with passages from the bible. It was not until much later that the farmer's wife recalled this detail and began to suspect that the old beggar was in fact a witch.

By that time, of course, things had gone ill indeed on the farm, for the cattle would grow sick and drop dead, one right after the other, until it was clear that the husband and wife would be doomed to lose their home if something could not be done. Experts were consulted of all kinds, and the property was walked carefully to look for anything that may have poisoned the cattle, but no clear cause could be found.

Eventually, they called a conjuror to them who was quite famous for discerning and abating black magic, and he rather quickly determined that the farm had indeed been cursed. His countercharm was simple, if grotesque; the calf that died most recently must be cut open, and its heart removed, for even briefly after death, the heart still held on to the witch's curse and thereby held a magical connection to the witch. The organ should be roasted over a fire, then pierced with iron nails, one right after the other.

And this was carried out by the farmer and his wife as the conjuror watched and guided, and as soon as the third nail pierced the heart, there came the old beggar woman, who was sweating and wide-eyed, wincing in terrible pain. The conjuror snatched the heart so as to hide it in his jacket, and he observed rather quickly that when he removed a nail, the old beggar seemed to breathe easier for a time, and when he stuck a nail in, she would groan and hold her chest in pain.

Eventually, the woman asked the man and wife if they could please spare some potatoes once more, for though she had been denied the last time, she was willing, she said, to "forget the whole matter" if they could part with even one. The conjuror nodded approvingly, and they sent her off with a single potato from their cellar, for which she thanked them, though not warmly.

No more of their cattle took illness after that, and indeed, the ones who were struck with the wasting curse improved day after day, until their farm was quite saved. And with the curse removed, the witch also recovered from the pains in her chest, and the conjuror saw no need to pursue the matter further, recommending only that the couple endeavor, perhaps, to be more generous to strangers in the future.

The Old Stone Road
New World

A very long time ago, along the old stone road between Brantford and Langford, which lies between the Great Lakes, there lived a blacksmith and his wife. Due to their location, they found the majority of their business in shoeing horses, for many travelers and merchants would come by the old road, and its rocky condition was difficult. Because this business became so frequent, the blacksmith stationed his assistant in a little cabin off the road, so that folks who needed emergency shoeing in the dead of night could knock upon his door.

One day, the blacksmith's assistant interrupted him and angrily announced that he was at last leaving his employment to go find work elsewhere.

The blacksmith was baffled by this. "Why would you leave now?" he asked him. "Have I done something that would keep you from staying?"

"You abuse me," said the young man, "for I am stationed there beside the road, and the work each night is endless. A man comes every hour, bringing one horse after another, and I spend all of my nightly hours shoeing his many horses, and all of my daytime hours helping you, and I am utterly spent."

The blacksmith found this strange, of course, and decided to meet this strange rider and speak with him himself, so he asked the young man to sleep in his own house for the night, so that any guests would be compelled to find him there. The young assistant slept on the floor by the fire, and the blacksmith on the couch so as to watch for visitors, and the blacksmith's wife slept alone in their bedroom.

No sooner had they all retired than a knock came at the door. The assistant, being so deprived of sleep, did not wake at the knock, and the blacksmith thought it best that he rest himself, of course, and so he went alone to answer the door. There in his doorway stood a man with a very fine-looking mare, a horse which seemed to him familiar somehow, though he could not place the memory.

"Would you shoe my horse, sir?" asked the man at the door, "for I've many miles to go yet."

And the blacksmith knew that this must be the man who had come so often and deprived his assistant of his sleep. "We are a busy place, sir," said the blacksmith, "and we need our sleep at night. You must go on your way."

"Please," begged the stranger, "won't you reconsider? I'll pay you five dollars for your trouble, if you will only shoe the front feet. And I'll bother you no more after that."

Although the blacksmith wanted to turn the man away, this was a considerable sum in those days, and the temptation was too great, so he agreed and did the job. The mare, however, acted very strangely the whole time, staring into his eyes, then following him around and nudging him, as if trying to tell the man something.

At any rate, the job was done at last, and the man mounted the horse and rode on his way, and left them the rest of the night in peace, for which the blacksmith was thankful, for he was eager to tell his assistant that the matter was over and he had no need to leave his employment.

The next morning, the blacksmith and assistant enjoyed breakfast together and talked about the strange man at length, how odd his looks and mannerisms were, and how glad they both were to be done with the affair. After a while, however, they noticed that the blacksmith's wife was absent, and upon visiting her room, the husband found his wife still in bed, weeping under her blankets.

He went to kiss her as he always did, and he noticed that she was covered in sweat and very pale, with dark circles under her eyes, as if from lack of sleep. His eye fell at last on something more troubling, for the edge of the bedsheet was stained red with blood. "Oh, wife!" he cried out, pulling back the blankets gently, and what he saw horrified him, for horseshoes had been nailed to both of her hands, and dried bloodstains were all over the bedsheets.

"But what has happened to you, wife? Who did this?" cried the blacksmith.

"Oh!" replied his wife in her misery, "It was a witch-man who rode me up and down the old stone road all night. And he brought me to you, and I begged for your help. But it was you, husband, who nailed these horseshoes to my hands."

The Devil's Yarn
Cornwall

Long ago, quite longer than anyone can remember, there lived a young woman named Duffy. Her father and stepmother claimed the girl was lazy and idle beyond all measure, and by most accounts, it was true. She was absent-minded by nature, and could never attend to her chores—not the cooking, the cleaning, the knitting, or the spinning. "Not even the Devil and his witches would keep such a lazy girl in their home," her stepmother would say.

It so happened one day that a squire was passing through the village, and on riding past, he heard the stepmother and daughter arguing loudly. The stepmother was, as usual, scolding Duffy's idleness, but on seeing the squire perched on his horse just at their door, the girl turned to him and proclaimed loudly, so that he might hear, "Don't believe my stepmother, your honor! My spinning is the best in all the parish."

"How fortunate," replied the squire, "for I'm much in need of a servant for my own home to help my housekeeper with all of the spinning."

The girl's stepmother laughed a hearty laugh, but she sent the girl along with the squire then, wishing him better luck with her than she had got. And he brought her to his fine house in the countryside and introduced her to his housekeeper, and they prepared for her a clean and comfortable room of her own.

And it was quite soon after this that Duffy realized the situation she was in, that she would be expected to spin wool better than anyone in the parish, and that if she were unable to do so, she would find herself turned out, and her stepmother would surely not take her back.

"Curse the spinning," Duffy said to herself in her chambers, seeing no answer to her woes. "The Devil may spin for the squire for all I care." It was then that a little man appeared in her chamber, dressed all in black, emerging from the pool of darkness in one corner of the room to approach her.

"I shall do the spinning," said the little man in black. "And someday, a lady you shall be. But in three years' time, I shall call you, and you shall come with me to Hell."

Now, being young and eager and perhaps less than wise, Duffy agreed to these terms, and the compact was made between them. And the little man in black spun such fine yarn that night that the girl was quite amazed. And he came again each night thereafter, and soon the squire and the entire town were impressed with the girl's skills, and her yarns and knits became so popular that all wanted to buy them, and before long she was invited to all manner of parties and gatherings and grew quite popular, so beloved that the squire himself decided he could not let some other man have her for his wife, and so he married her himself.

In those days, Duffy was quite happy, and she attended gatherings hosted by the miller and his wife, who went by the name of Bet, and who was known to be a witch of considerable skill. And as the two became close, the witch half-suspected that poor Duffy was under some unfair compact with a spirit, but she did not want to accuse her friend of such things, and so she held her tongue.

A long while passed, until one night, realizing that her three years were nearly spent, Duffy pleaded with the little man in black. Her eyes full of tears, she told him that she would give anything to stay with her beloved husband in her comfortable home, that she would do all of the spinning herself from then on if need be, and that she was sorry for troubling him so needlessly to do all this work.

The little Devil was moved then, as much as he could be at least, for he offered Duffy the chance to earn her freedom. "If you can guess my name before thy time is up," he said, "then I'll not take thee to Hell."

It was several nights later, after many unsuccessful rounds of guessing, that Duffy went to her friend Bet, and to the kind witch, she at last confided her troubles. "I've had my share of dealings with the imps of darkness," said the witch. "And if you'll do as I say, all will be well, but mind you follow my advice perfectly, and trust me as much as you can."

The witch Bet directed the girl to bring her some very good whisky that day, and later that evening, to send her husband, the squire, to the edge of the woods, where he was to wait and watch silently. And all of this she did, and Duffy sat in her house nervously waiting for what her husband would say when he returned home.

When at last he arrived, the squire was terribly drunk. He barged through the door, dancing wildly, and singing at the top of his lungs:

> *Here's to the Devil,*
> *With his wooden pick and shovel,*
> *Digging tin by the bushel*
> *With his tail cocked up!*

But Duffy calmed him, and at last got him to sit and drink water, and he told her all that had happened that night.

He told her how he saw Bet, the miller's wife, leading a company of witches through the forest, how they stirred and conjured a great blue fire in a ring, how a little Devil dressed in black appeared there in the flames, how he kissed each one of them and danced with them in the darkness, how the squire himself felt compelled to join them in their revels, and how they welcomed him and danced with him, how he wondered if he might wish to be a witch himself, how Bet produced from her cloak a bottle of whisky by which they all got thoroughly drunk, and how the Devil began dancing on his own, drunkenly and wildly, laughing and yelling at the top of his lungs:

> *The foolish girl! The foolish girl!*
> *Thy Devil's name be Terrytop!*

And so Duffy kissed her husband and wrapped her arms around him, for though he did not know it, he had saved her from being taken down to Hell. And when her friend Bet, the clever witch, came at last to join them, she kissed her on the cheek, for she had given her back her freedom.

When the little man in black appeared to her that night, which was the last night of her contract, Duffy greeted him by his own name, Terrytop. He was, as one might guess, quite taken aback by this, for he did not surmise the girl capable of ever guessing his true name. "I suppose," said the little Devil after a long pause, "that Hell can wait a bit longer. For one day, we will have all of eternity together, after all."

The Black Crane
Scotland

In olden times, the prophecies of witching folk were serious matters indeed, consulted by peasants and chiefs alike for guidance in all matters of dire importance to one's livelihood, and indeed, one's very life. And so it was that Ewen Maclaine of the Isle of Mull consulted a well-known witch for guidance on the eve before a great battle with a neighboring chief.

But the prophecies of witching folk are tricky things as well, for they seldom deal in absolutes. More often, the prophecy offers contingencies—tasks that must be fulfilled in order to achieve one outcome or the other. In matters of fate, even the most mundane acts may alter the course of events in great and terrible ways.

The witch was invited to Maclaine's house in Lochbuie, where Ewen and his wife and all of the men to fight in the battle the next day had gathered to hear her words. The witch's foretelling was this: should Maclaine's wife prepare a meal for him and his men without being asked to do so, the battle would be won. Should she not, or should she do so only after being asked, the battle would be lost, and their deaths would be all but assured. On hearing these words, the men's eyes fell coldly on Maclaine's wife, for she was well-known to be cruel and heartless.

And indeed, it was the simple matter of breakfast that proved Maclaine's undoing. The next morning, despite knowing the dread words of the prophecy, his wife had prepared no food for the men at all. This was, of course, no mere slight or slip of memory, but an intentional act of malice to bring about their deaths. We know little, of course, of the lady's own motives; perhaps she had endured much in life, so much that, at last, her heart was turned to stone against them all.

In any case, Maclaine demanded that she feed them something, forgetting the words of the prophecy, that the meal must be prepared for them *unasked*. His wife brought them only curds, without even spoons to eat them with. Maclaine was of course furious, and the hearts of his men sank, and their faces turned long and dour, for they knew then that the day would bring their deaths.

"How then, wife, are we to eat without spoons?" asked Ewen Maclaine.

The lady smirked then, pleased with her own malice. "Perhaps with the bills of birds," she answered coldly, gazing out over all of those doomed men. And it was this cruel joke that earned her the nickname of *Corr-dhu*, or *The Black Crane*, a moniker by which she was known for the rest of her life and for generations after.

While the men managed to eat some of the curds using only their hands to scoop and feed themselves, Maclaine ate none, seemingly resigned to his fate and unwilling to let his last meal become a demeaning show for the Corr-dhu's amusement.

But the strange twist of the tale is this: for while Maclaine and many of his men did die in battle on the Isle of Mull that day, his ghost was seen long after, for to die unfed before a battle is a terrible thing, and it is said that Ewen Maclaine still roams on horseback, searching for his last meal, a fate that was, despite the witch's prophecy, sealed by his own wife, who was surely haunted and tormented for the rest of her days.

That ghost is still seen, they say, by descendants bearing the Maclaine name. And so, if you are of the Maclaine line, dear reader, and you happen to be visited by a wounded and hungry-looking man on horseback, perhaps consider offering what you can in kindness, lest this spirit think you cruel and black-hearted, like the Corr-dhu, and unleash his wrath upon you as well.

Besom and Crossroads
Isle of Man

Once, long ago, though not so long as to be in ancient times, there was a man traveling by road in the parish of Andreas on the Isle of Man. It was May Eve, which is famously a night of witchcraft, and as he was traveling, he came across an old crossroads, and he saw there one of his neighbors, a woman reputed by the locals to be a true witch.

Using her besom, she had swept a great ring about her, which was tremendous in size, cut into three segments by the crossroads. The woman was calling out to dark powers, spirits of torment and suffering, and so he approached her and warned her to cease, at which she scoffed.

Three nights this happened; each time, the man traveled again by night past the old crossroads, only to find the witch once more standing in the midst of her swept circle, performing her dark conjurations to injure her enemies. At last, the man had had enough, and so, on the third night, he took her broom from her, and dashed away, ignoring her threats in the distance. And with the broom now in his own two hands, he noticed that it was a strange thing indeed. Woven into its bristles was a curious cord of some kind, with a length of seventeen knots.

Later, with the aid of some local farmhands, he set a great pyre of gorse, and into that red fire, he cast the witch's besom. As it burned and crackled, it is said that it made a series of great sounds, which echoed across the distance, like a gun being fired again and again. Soon after, the witch was found dead in her home, for burning the besom with the knotted cord had turned her own dark witchery back upon her.

The Witch-Wood Charm
New World

They say that once, at the foot of a steep mountain somewhere near the Connecticut River, there lived a woman who was plagued by the witches both night and day. What she had done to incur their wrath is a matter of speculation. Perhaps she had accidentally wandered upon their secret meeting on some moonlit night, or perhaps she had spoken ill of some witch-neighbor or denied them aid in a time of need. Such things do happen.

In any case, the woman would often be seen outside her cabin at the foot of the mountain, shouting at the witches, attempting to cast them off of her land, but to no avail. She claimed to anyone who would listen that the spirits of the witches would visit her at night to torment her in various inhuman forms, sometimes sending other dark spirits to do their work for them. Most thought her touched in the head and did not believe her—at least, until her death.

You see, the mountain woman had for years worn a special charm around her neck, a talisman which she claimed protected her from being murdered by the witches, and though it did not prevent them from plaguing her with their visits at all hours, she credited her perseverance through this torment to this very object. It was made of the wood of the mountain ash, an American tree sometimes called witch-wood, which is similar in form to the rowan tree. As long as the woman wore this charm, she had claimed, the witches could not actually lay their hands on her, try as they might.

Eventually, after living a long, though unfortunate life, she was found dead one day outside her home, the talisman still around her neck. She appeared to have died carrying water from a well, which was not in itself suspicious, since she was of a very advanced age.

What was strange, however, was what happened when the witch-wood charm was removed from her neck. The moment it was taken from her, there suddenly appeared bruises all over her body in the shape of handprints—many slender handprints, as if made by hands with very long fingers.

Black Paternosters
Scotland

Agnes Sampson, a well-known healer and midwife commonly referred to as the "Wise-Wife of Keith," was accused of witchcraft in the late sixteenth century. She was said to have healed her clients by taking their ailment into herself, then "casting it" upon an animal, which would waste away with the sickness while the patient grew healthier day by day. She was also said to make use of powders ground together from strange ingredients, which she would give to patients, particularly women in labor, in order to soothe pain.

The wise-wife was believed to possess two spoken charms that were dear to her, a Black Paternoster and a White Paternoster, both of these being amalgamations of Catholic prayer and practical magic that she used for protection and blessing. Such "Paternosters" are, in fact, legendary charms of frequent appearance in Scottish witch lore, though their forms vary considerably. Some say there exist Green Paternosters, Red Paternosters, and even Blue Paternosters as well.

It was in the late 1500s that Hector Munro, the 17th Baron of Foulis, was accused of witchcraft. In the course of his trial, he too was accused of using a "Paternoster" charm, this being the Black Paternoster, which he was believed to have used with clippings of hair and nails and water enchanted by magical stones in order to affect the death of his own brother. Most versions of the Black Paternoster left to us today are protective in nature, so while the existence of such charms was very real and known, the intended use here seems to be represented in a twisted fashion so as to hasten a conviction.

Today, of course, one of the most famous of the Black Paternosters is still in existence, albeit in the form of a children's prayer, beginning with the famous lines, "Now I lay me down to sleep. / I pray the Lord my soul to keep." Its origins belie its appearance, for though it is a much-changed version of only one iteration of the Paternoster tapestry, it did, in fact, originate in witch-lore as a spoken charm.

Witch's Legs
Ireland

Once, long ago, on a still and dark evening much like this one, a clergyman was traveling at night on horseback. In those days, traveling alone at night was a frightful thing. But he had been summoned to attend to the last rites of a dying man in a neighboring town, and with prayer at his lips, he steeled himself against the shadows that played along the brush and behind the trees, fearing no evil in the name of the Lord to whom he had devoted his life.

Upon crossing an old bridge laid over a rushing creek, his horse began behaving strangely, tossing its head and glancing at the nearby edge of the woods, as if carefully watching something the priest could not see. He calmed the horse and went along his journey.

Going past a great, twisted tree upon a hill, the horse took fright again, resisting its rider and whinnying in the silence of the night, as if to say it would go no further. He soothed the creature once more, and eventually consoled it enough that the horse allowed them to continue the journey.

Just as the priest crossed by a great old stone, which meant that he was only a short ride from his destination, the horse became terribly vexed, resisting all attempts to travel any further. Its eyes darted wildly at the thickets all around them, and then at last to the road before them, where the priest finally saw what his horse had been afraid of all the while.

Walking down the road through the trees, as calmly and nimbly as you please, was a pair of human legs cut off at the waist, with no torso, arms, or head attached to them. The thing wore a pair of buckskin britches, and where they ended, its hairy legs were covered with muck from its journey through the mud of the roadsides.

Remembering his faith, the priest steadied himself and spoke to the figure directly. "Good evening, fine sir, and whither are you going without your shoes?"

The figure spoke not a word, but stopped walking and stood silently.

"Not a talkative one, I see. Of course, without a head, I imagine the courtesies of speech must elude you often."

Again, the figure spoke not.

"Enough of this, creature. What manner of spirit are you, and what witch or devil has sent you upon this night?"

Still, the figure spoke not a word.

"Very well," said the priest grimly. "Perhaps a taste of my whip will hurry your answer." And with that, he delivered a great lashing upon the thing, and it stumbled and fell.

At that very moment, and to the priest's great surprise, there welled up from the soil around the roadside what appeared to be milk, enough milk to pool and pour over his horse's hooves. The priest delivered another blow, and again, milk seeped up from the earth, pouring over the path as if from a flood. With the third lashing, there was so much milk that it came halfway up the horse's legs, rushing over the whole hillside and down the trail.

When the great flood of milk subsided, there lay on the road a woman the priest knew but in passing. She groaned and writhed in torment, but her eyes darted rage.

"Sarah," said the priest, "long have I urged you to leave behind your wicked ways and return to the embrace of the church. But it is clear to me this night that you have turned thoroughly to witchcraft." And with that, the witch passed from this world.

When the priest returned home, he called upon several men to gather up the woman's body and return it to her cottage to be mourned and buried. He learned from the townsfolk that the witch had but one cow, but sold more butter than anyone in the county, especially when the cows of neighboring farms refused, quite mysteriously, to give any milk at all.

Though the witch was not well-loved in the community, she was survived by a daughter every bit as strange in her ways as her mother, and the girl is said to have made a new home somewhere under a new name. For the rest of his days, the priest refused to travel the countryside at night, for he could not erase from his mind the cold gaze of the woman lying on the roadside in her final moments, nor could he help but think of the witch's daughter waiting for her vengeance somewhere out there in the dark.

Granny Cobb
New World

Not all witching folk of the old tales are of the same ilk or persuasion. Some work a dark craft, tormenting others for their own benefit or amusement. Others seek to heal or aid those around them, protecting them from harm. Most, of course, are both, or something in between.

It happened in New England once, a very long time ago, that a young girl named Libby was plagued by a witch's curse. At first, the symptoms were subtle. She would swear that she could see someone in the room who wasn't there, or that she felt someone touch her gently on the shoulder when there was no one around the girl. These spells became more serious, though, when she began going into fits, screaming that the witch was upon her. She would shake violently, jumping up and down, slamming herself into walls, even harming herself with whatever she could find. Once, she broke into a fit so violent that her parents tied her to a kitchen chair, at which the entire chair lifted off the ground, a frightening sight that could not be explained. It was then that the mother decided to call upon a witching man, a charmer who specialized in removing curses, to come to the girl's aid.

The man eventually came, and after assessing the girl's condition, handed the mother a small charm, telling her to set it boiling in a pot of water on the stove, that its influence might deter the witch's spirit from entering. But no sooner had the water come to a boil than the girl went into a more violent fit than ever before, thrashing about like an animal, jumping higher than any human being should be capable of, until at last, she screamed aloud, "The witch Granny Cobb is upon me, and she will have me soon!" The girl then ran to the kitchen and pressed her hands upon the boiling pot, burning herself badly, and then falling unconscious.

The witching man's eyes narrowed at this event. He was not afraid, but was clearly frustrated by the witch's powerful hold on the girl. "Set the girl to rest in bed," he said, "and give me leave to use your cellar as I will. I'll speak with the witch myself."

The mother and father sat at their table, which was just above where the cellar lay beneath, listening carefully so as to make out what was happening below. They heard the witching man's familiar voice calling out strange words in the dark of the cellar. He called out the same phrase several times, and though they could not make out the words themselves, it was clear that this was some kind of question being posed.

Finally, he called out the same query a third time, louder and angrier than before, and the voice that spoke back to him was someone else's, not of his own, for it was deep and hollow and full of hatred, and this second voice so frightened the mother and father that they held each other in terror.

The witching man could be heard to reply this time in plain English, saying, "Will you leave the girl alone, or no?"

"She'll be mine until the day I die," said the hollow voice in reply.

"A promise you will keep," said the witching man, and such a scream was heard after that—a scream like neither the mother nor the father had ever heard in their lives, both human and animal, echoing through the house, into the darkness of the night.

The next morning, Libby awoke, seemingly free of her mysterious illness. She claimed that she could feel the witch Granny Cobb no more, that the bond between them had somehow been broken. She soon returned to a state of health, just as she was before the affliction. And not long after, the witch Granny Cobb was found lying dead in her own home, for she was indeed a local woman who lived several miles away, and she had been suspected of dark craft for a very long time.

Milk and Feathers
England

Many witches throughout history rose to a level of prestige and legend due to the usefulness of their skills to their community, often becoming highly sought-after and locally famous for their witchery. Such is the case of old Nan Barrett, a quite famous practitioner of the arts in the town of Eye, her specialty being fortune-telling and the finding of lost objects and livestock.

One day, a woman came to old Nan's cottage seeking her aid in locating her lost stock of feathers, which were quite important in those days, for they were used in crafting all manner of useful things, from beds to pillows to quills. Old Nan told her that the feathers would return, and she need fret no more, and pleased with this augury, the woman paid the witch and left. On her way out the door, however, she heard old Nan chuckle to herself, saying that the feathers would indeed return, but that the woman would not be glad of it.

On returning home, the woman tasked her household with other chores, for there was much milking to be done, and she decided to let the matter of the feathers go entirely, thinking herself wise to avoid the ill fortune old Nan had muttered as she left.

But as they set out the pails of fresh milk, the feathers drifted down from the hayloft, falling into every last pail, and ruining both the milk and the feathers at once. And from then on, the woman knew that it was not possible to avoid or outsmart the fate foretold by the witch Nan Barrett.

Three Knots of Wind
Scotland

Many ages and a great many generations ago, on the Isle of Harris, there lived a boatman who had fallen in love with a witch's daughter. Although there are many tales of witches who punish suitors for being unworthy of their children, this was not the case in this instance, for the girl's witch-mother accepted the man and genuinely cared for him. Whether he was worthy of that family, though, is another matter.

It happened once that the boatman was detained by adverse winds, which prevented him from setting sail from the island in order to transport his goods. Eventually, he approached his sweetheart's witch-mother for aid. It was known then, and is still known among some, that witches of the islands of Scotland can bind the wind in knots so that boatmen may release a gale when they need one. This was the charm he asked of the witch-mother, a favor to which she agreed.

And so the witches of the island all congregated at the request of the girl's witch-mother, and they at last all commenced to put their magical powers together to aid the man. After three days of long charm-work, they produced a spelled cord with three knots tied thereon, and on giving it over to her would-be son-in-law, the witch imparted to him the instructions for its use. The first knot was called, she said, *Come gently.* When untied, it would conjure a soft breeze. The second knot was called *Come better*, and when untied, it would conjure a stiff gale. The third knot was called *Hardship*, and he was not to undo the last one except in dire straits, for it would rip the thatch from houses and blow down the very hills to rubble.

But of course, the young man being a fool, he did not heed the witch's instructions. As soon as he stepped onto his boat, he untied one knot after another, rapidly and eagerly, for he wished to embark on a swift course and make up for the money he had lost due to being trapped on the island for days. He had just made it off of the docks, and the tempest began to rage around him as he feverishly untied the knots, and it was only by his good fortune that the other boatmen were able to draw the boat back by rope before he was able to fully untie the last knot, which would have killed them all.

Though he did survive, one wonders whether the witch could still bless her daughter's choice of husband after that day. For what self-respecting witch would accept such a simple fool for a son-in-law?

A Witch-Hare
Wales

In the Welsh village of Drws-y-Nant, a very long time ago, there lived a servant girl in a small but stable household who would spend her day tending to such variety of everyday chores as needed and assigned by the family. Now, there had been talk in the village lately of witches—of strange sightings, ill omens, and evidence of witchcraft worked upon the local farming families, but the girl paid these no mind, for she did not believe in such things.

On one particular morning, she was set to churning butter, which was her least favorite of all her regular chores. The other servants were attending to various matters around the estate, and so the girl was left alone in the kitchen with the old churn, the door open so that the breeze might freshen the room. After working the churn for hours, she became very tired and frustrated, for no butter would come, and churning is, of course, quite hard work. No matter how long she churned, the cream would not set, and no butter would form at all. The weather was unseasonably hot, and she decided to stop and rest for a bit and think.

When she returned to the task, she decided to inspect the milk once more, and as she looked within the old churn, which had proved reliable for years, she noticed something strange. Under the glossy, white surface of the milk, something appeared to be moving and writhing. She reached in with a clean hand to feel, and what she felt was a living creature, warm and slippery, its hair slick with milk. With a great splash, the thing leapt out from the churn then, and the girl could see that it was a wild hare. The thing scampered just outside the door to the kitchen, then stopped and stared her squarely in the eyes, its fur quite matted and dripping with milk.

The girl knew that this was a witch-hare for sure, for in that part of the country, witches loved the shape of the hare best of all. This meant, of course, that the rumors about the village had been true. And the presence of the witch-hare could mean only one thing: that a witch somewhere nearby was stealing the butter from the farm, and who knows what else besides, for such forms of dark craft are worked by those who desire the prosperity of others, and would have it for themselves at any cost. The creature stared at her eerily from a distance with its wild, golden eyes, and all of the birds and insects and sounds of nature fell silent, and the wind went still, and the air felt heavier around her than before.

It was then that the girl remembered an old bit of lore that her mother had passed on to her in her younger years: that evil witches, like malevolent faeries, could be warded off with iron. She took up an old rusted nail, which had come loose from a board nearby, and clutched it firmly in her hand, making the sign of the cross. At this, the creature scampered off and away, presumably to some other important business of witchery.

What became of the servant girl after that, we cannot say. If she was wise, perhaps she made use of other protective implements of craft her mother surely taught her—the broom hung above the door, or whitethorn twigs, or any of the other old charms to guard against evil witchery. Such things exist for a purpose, after all, and should be well remembered.

Devil Take Me, Ring and All
New World

Old man Ferro was a witching man, that much was known. He could curse a hunter's rifle so that it could never again hit wild game, or he could fix your cow so that it would never again give milk. He knew remedies and signs, too, old ways to heal and to preserve life when he wished to do so. All the folks in Ashe County, North Carolina feared old man Ferro with a terrible fear—everyone, that is, but a young man by the name of Eph Tucker.

Young Eph was possessed of a strong desire to become a witching man himself. He longed for others to fear him the way they feared old man Ferro. After all, when a witching man wanted a jug of milk or a sack of flour, all he needed to do was ask, and some farmer or other would oblige him respectfully, often in the hopes of earning his favor for some help down the road, but more often out of fear of being cursed. It was this sort of life for which young Eph longed, and if becoming a witch was the way to get it, then so be it.

After a great deal of deliberation, Eph decided to approach old man Ferro himself and ask him how he might become a witch. The old man was difficult, particularly when in a foul mood, but nothing would prevent young Eph from seeking his prize. And so he decided to set out one morning to make the journey on horseback through the dark wood, which would take most of the day.

The journey was long, but before he knew it, night was on its way. Dark was quickly enfolding the wooded hills, but the young man pressed on until he saw the smokestacks of a small cabin, where he tied his horse and went to knock upon the door. Finding it slightly ajar, he let himself in, and there was old man Ferro, seated upon a rocking chair beside the fireplace, gazing into its embers.

"I know what you've come for, boy," said the old witchman, gravely. "And I know you'll not be turned away until I tell you how to become a witch yourself."

"I'm ready. Tell me then," said Eph, eagerly.

"We'll need a quiet place out in the woods. Follow me, and I'll show you what to do."

The two made their way by lantern light up a small hill behind the cabin. As they walked, Eph could hear the sounds of sticks breaking around them, as if something were following along, and once or twice, he could have sworn he saw someone moving in the distance in pace with their footsteps.

Finally, they came to a little clearing in the trees, and old man Ferro set down his lantern there. He reached into the brush and broke off a great, crooked stick, then began tracing a circle in the cold dirt. The woods had grown chilly in the night, and young Eph shivered.

"Stand in the middle, boy," said Ferro.

Young Eph did as he was told, though a great fear was upon him now.

"Lay down there in the dirt on your side, with your knees to your chest. Put one hand on the bottom of your right foot, and put the other on top of your head."

Young Eph did as he was told, though his hands trembled. The cracking sounds around them had grown louder now, and he was sure that there was someone or something else with them in the woods.

"Now, repeat after me, boy: *Devil take me, ring and all.*"

"Devil t-take me," stammered young Eph, who was thoroughly shook with terror, "ring and—"

Before he could finish saying the words, young Eph felt the ground sink underneath him, as if he were being swallowed up by the very earth, and he felt many hands around him, touching him all over. He went into a wild state then, pale and screaming, and ran frantically back towards the cabin and his horse. He could hear old man Ferro cackling behind him loudly, mocking his horror. He mounted his horse and rode as swiftly as he ever had, and he did not stop until he reached town the next day.

They say young Eph never did become a witch properly, but that was perhaps for the best, in the end. He took a job at a nearby farm, and in the years to come, married and had children of his own and enjoyed all of the conventional sorts of happiness that were, it turns out, better suited to his nature.

The Witch of Treva
Cornwall

In the village of Treva, in Zennor parish, it is said that there once lived a powerful witch who was both respected and feared by the townsfolk. Folks said she was capable of casting terrible curses, of ruining one's land or livestock, and so all were careful not to give her any offense or any reason at all to dislike them.

Her husband, however, did not believe such tales, and he could not understand for the life of him how so many of his neighbors were afraid of his wife, for he spoke to her however he pleased, and often harshly, and no harm had come to him yet. One night, after a long day's work, the man was terribly hungry, and he demanded that his witch-wife prepare him a meal of meat and tatties. "I cannot get meat from a stone," she said to him in reply, at which he flew into a rage.

"Aren't you the all-powerful witch of Treva?" he yelled, mockingly. "Haven't you all the powers of the Old One at your disposal? Go and get me some meat to eat, and quick, or else I'll be the death of you."

The witch of Treva said no words of protest, nor did she respond to his threats, but quietly and calmly walked right past him, as if he were nothing to her then, and on her way out the door, her shape twisted and bent and grew dark, and she became a hare with long ears and wild eyes, and the hare scampered off into the distance. The man was suddenly struck with fear, but watched on, and after several moments, he saw his own wife walking back down the road towards their cottage, carrying a great platter of meat and potatoes.

His witch-wife walked past him again, cold and expressionless, and she set the platter on the table, but the man was no longer hungry. "Eat, husband," she commanded him sternly, and he did so, just as he was told. And dear reader, though we cannot say for certain what manner of witchcraft went into that meal, it is said that her husband lived in fear of her for the rest of his days, never speaking another word against her or raising his voice to her in any circumstance, and she was from that day forward the utter ruler of that household in all things.

And when, many decades later, the witch of Treva finally passed from this world, they say that the room around her deathbed grew dark, and that many spirits with whom she had consorted could be heard, for they had all gathered together at once to be with her in her passing. Their voices echoed about the room, and dark forms could be seen moving from one corner to the next, and these spirits, which had been loyal to her in life, stayed with her until her last breath.

At her funeral, she was carried to the churchyard by six pallbearers, as was the custom, and there are those who swear that a hare appeared out of nowhere, leaping over the coffin, terrifying everyone present. And when the coffin was set down for a moment, a cat leapt upon it, and perched there for a bit, staring squarely at the men before going on its way. When at last, they placed the coffin in a fresh grave, and the parson reached that portion of the burial service that contains the words, *I am the resurrection and the life*, a witch-hare appeared on the edge of the churchyard, and as it opened its mouth, it let out a deep howl such that no earthly creature could make, then shifted into an enormous, shadowy figure, and disappeared into the trees.

If the old lore is a teacher, we might wonder whether a witch of such abilities can truly die a death as we know it. Perhaps, in her mastery of old, dark powers, the witch of Treva discovered the means to life in some other form. In which case, she probably did not care for the parson's recitation of his own beliefs about resurrection.

The Cursing Bone
Scotland

Among the many antiquities preserved in the collections of the National Museums of Scotland, one may come across a particularly strange object catalogued as a *charm*: a length of hollow bone, which appears to be wedged into a hole bored in a diamond-shaped piece of bog oak. Held upright, the thing would look like the shape of a skewed cross, but its legendary history is anything but Christian. In fact, its popular name has become "the witch's cursing bone."

This object was contributed to the museum collections by Lady Elspeth Campbell, daughter of the tenth Duke of

Argyll, sometime in the early 1900s, though it was quite old at the time it was donated. It comes from the Argyll region on the western side of Scotland, specifically Glen Shira. The entire Argyll region is known for its witchery, for in the old days, the witches of that place were quite famous for the potency of their craft, especially for workings of vengeance and cursing.

The legend, which was passed along by Lady Elspeth Campbell, says that the bone was used by an infamous witch of the local area. When she wished to "ill-will" or curse an enemy, she would go out under the cover of darkness to her victim's property, making her way to the hen-house. There, she would identify the hen that sat closest to the rooster, the one that he loved best.

Finally, she would wring the hen's neck, twisting the head off its body, and pouring its blood through the hollow center of the bone where the marrow had once been. This was performed while uttering the necessary spoken curses aimed at the enemy. The witch's victim, whoever it may be, was then "ill-willed," as surely as the hen's blood flowed through the cursing bone and onto the cold ground.

The Burning Cauldron
Isle of Man

It happened long ago that a baron from Norway had taken up residence on the Isle of Man, which was, at the time, full of wild game. Deer and elk were numerous on the island, and hunters were quite careful to take only what they needed so that those populations could renew themselves, and so all could partake in a bit of hunting, an unspoken rule abided out of fairness for all.

The baron, however, had no respect for this tradition. They say that he hunted the wild elk with an endless obsession, being gone for many days and nights on end, and that much of the meat and hides were left to waste, for he had no need of these, nor any intention of using them at all. And all of this ceaseless hunting eventually resulted in the complete extinction of elk on the island.

It is at this point in the story that a very famous witch-wife by the name of Ada heard of this matter. She heard, too, of his plans to embark the very next day to sail home to Norway, after which, on his return, he would begin a great hunt for red deer, which would surely result in the same unfortunate end, leaving no red deer on the island for anyone else to hunt.

After the baron had set sail the next day, the witch-wife Ada set off on an expedition of her own. She went to the kitchens of the baron's castle, for only the cook was left behind when he went on his hunt, and from a distance, she charmed the great cooking cauldron over the fire so that the fat bubbled over on one side, spilling onto the flames, and setting the great castle ablaze. At this, the cook screamed so loudly that the baron heard him from many miles in the distance on his ship, and looking across the waves, he saw his own castle wreathed in red flame.

Of course, the baron ordered the ship to return so that he might intervene, but his panic and rage at the sight of his own castle burning clouded his good judgment. For he hastened the crew beyond sound reason, and the ship was wrecked upon rocks beneath the waves, and all aboard the vessel were drowned. And so the great baron was brought to ruin and death, not by a great and terrible curse or the conjuration of dark spirits, but by a simple charm cast on a cooking pot.

Pins and Pig Livers
New World

Somewhere in the wilds of Ontario, long ago, it happened that a small company was gathered together for dinner at the home of an elderly man called Uncle Simon, who had served as a soldier in his younger days, and was well-loved by many a neighbor.

As they dined and drank, filling the evening with stories and recollections and laughter, he himself told a strange tale. He said that just the other week, he had attempted to purchase some pigs from a neighbor woman who had refused his offer. The old man grew visibly angry as he spoke of it. He said it was no matter though, for the old woman would very soon regret turning him away. This struck the company as a strange thing to say, but they carried on with their evening nonetheless, attributing the odd statement to his age or to the drink.

After some time, though, their host was suddenly seized with terrible pains and became quite pale and visibly ill. He fell to the floor, contorting his body and gripping his vital organs, and then, quite suddenly, fell dead. No one knew what to make of this, but one among the company suggested that perhaps witchcraft was at work, and that they should go to the home of the woman who refused the sale of her pigs to see if perhaps the man had been spelled.

Upon arriving at the woman's home, they found her table covered with pigs' livers, stretched out and bloody and reeking. The organs had been stuck through with all manner of pins and needles, such that they looked like pincushions, and the woman was tossing them into a pot of boiling water, one by one. This scene horrified them, and they immediately accused her of witchcraft, for the old man had died gripping his vital organs just as if he had been lanced.

"A curse, a curse, you say?" replied the old woman, hot with rage, "a curse like the one that old Simon put on my pigs, simply because I refused to sell them? Why couldn't he leave them alone like I told him? This is no more than a curse returned, tit for tat."

And to that, the company had little to say, for it was well-known that a witch's curse held the signature of the witch, and that if old Uncle Simon had cursed the animals, then any harm done to their remains would be sent back upon the caster. In this, there was no doubt. Uncle Simon had been a witch-man all this time, and his own curse had been turned back on him by the cunning old woman.

To Ride the Devil
Scotland

Long ago, in the age of the legendary sorcerers of old Scotland, there lived a very great charmer by the name of Michael Scot. So great was his magical art that he was known throughout both the highlands and the lowlands, and when the people faced a problem that could not be solved by ordinary means, it was known that Michael Scot could succeed where others could not. His knowledge of science and the occult was legendary, and he was said to have many strange powers.

One of the ways the wizard was said to excel in his art was by means of a particular spirit at his disposal, for some said that Michael had succeeded, in the course of mastering his powers, in imprisoning the Devil himself and holding him captive as his own servant, conjuring him up anytime at all to enact his will as he so pleased. This was, on the one hand, a testament to his wits, for it is known that one must be quite sharp to outsmart the Devil. On the other hand, it was a testament to his dark power, for to command such a force made one a dangerous and capable sorcerer indeed.

It happened once that the Scottish people were much frustrated, for every year, they were forced to send word to Rome in order to determine the appointed dates of Shrovetide, the days leading up to Ash Wednesday and the Lenten season. Growing tired of this whole affair, it was decided that they should send for Michael Scot, that he might somehow simplify the thing and rid them of the needlessly complex task each year.

And so Michael Scot, they say, summoned up the Devil himself, and by his art, changed Old Hornie into a great black stallion, and they departed for Rome, so that Michael might corner the Pope himself and force his hand to simplify the whole matter such that the people would never be forced to write letters back and forth over the dates of Shrovetide again.

They rode a great distance, over both land and sea, and at a certain point, the Devil became tired and vexed by the journey, and he attempted to trick the sorcerer into releasing him to assume his own form. "What is it they say," asked the Devil, "when the women tuck their children into bed at night?"

"Never you mind. Ride on," replied Michael Scot. The Devil had, of course, hoped he would recite a nightly prayer, for if the sorcerer spoke of God or the saints, the spell by which they traveled would be broken.

"What is it they say, then," the Devil attempted a second time, "when the women rake their fire at the end of the evening?" Again, the Devil hoped that the charmer would mention God or the saints, for if he did so, the Old One could abandon the form of the magic horse, and Michael Scot would fall and drown in the sea.

But the wizard was clever, and he could not be duped by such a simple trick. "Never you mind what the women say, you wretch," he shouted at him boldly, giving the Devil a firm kick to remind him who his master was.

At last, they arrived in Rome, and it is said that when they came before the pope, they had soared at such a height on their travels that there was still snow on Michael's hat. The sorcerer noticed something quite unexpected, however, when glancing at the pope's feet, for on one of them was a lady's slipper, and it was evident that his holiness had been wearing women's shoes only a moment before, and had forgotten to remove both of them to greet his guest.

"You've snow on your hat," said the pope to Michael Scot. "How would a man ride so high, except by means of the dark arts?"

"And you've a lady's slipper on your foot," said Michael to the pope. "Perhaps, let's leave it there, and we shall keep each other's secrets, hmm?"

And at this, the old pope was surely at a loss, and so he agreed, and he divulged to the charmer the secret to determining the dates of Shrovetide, which is of course, as we all know today, inferred by where the new moon falls in the spring. And so Michael Scot was able to ride back to Scotland on his black stallion, which was the very Devil, in order to bring the people at last an answer to their vexation, and he and the pope stayed quite out of each other's way from that day on.

Cap and Rue
Ireland

A great many generations ago, longer than anyone can remember today, there lived a man named Seamus who kept in his employment an elderly woman and suspected witch by the name of Madge. The old woman was full of character and quite headstrong in her ways, but her work was good, and so Seamus kept old Madge on for many a year, and they generally got on in the way that people do who come to know one another's ways over time.

Now, each night, old Madge would prepare for Seamus a drought to help him sleep, for he was known to wake up in the night, and without this special drink from the old woman, he would find no rest whatsoever, but with her concoction, he would sleep like the dead and wake up well-rested. On one particular night, however, Seamus forgot to drink his drought, leaving it untouched beside his bed as he fell asleep.

He was awakened around midnight to the sound of laughing and singing, and he immediately lit his candle and made his way down through the house, following the sounds, until he came to the kitchen. There, seated around the kitchen table, sat a number of old women, and his housekeeper Madge among their company. They were loudly drinking and laughing and singing strange songs. So strange was this sight to him that Seamus decided to hide around a corner and watched them for a time.

"And to the great, wise, upright master of this house, sleeping like a fat hog in his bed even now!" toasted Madge, raising her glass high in the air, at which all of the other old women cackled and screeched in amusement.

One of the women who looked to be the oldest, her braids of gray hair so long they reached her legs, produced from her shawl a gnarled twig, and holding it out in front of her, said the strange words:

> *By yarrow and rue,*
> *And my red cap, too,*
> *Hie over to England!*

And no sooner were the words spoken than the old woman was whisked into the air and flew through the old fireplace and up the chimney, as if she were made of smoke.

One by one, then, the remaining women all repeated the charm, and all were whisked up the chimney like smoke, but when at last it came time for old Madge to fly herself away with the other witches, Seamus leapt forth from behind the corner and snatched the twig from her hand.

"Mock me in my sleep, will you?" snarled Seamus. "You distasteful old crocodile. Stay where you are, and if you're not here when I return, things will be even worse for you." Old Madge merely rolled her eyes and crossed her arms, of course, as was her way.

Then did Seamus speak the charm himself, and he found his twig transformed somehow into a steed, and he rode it through the whisps of smoke and gusts of wind and clouds, and he was very careful the whole time not to speak a single word, for it is known that to speak during witch-flight may break the spell if one is not careful.

On that dark and tumbling path through the air, Seamus was spun round and round, and he could not tell where he was going, until at last he was stopped abruptly and landed among the old witches' company in what appeared to be a cellar lit with small lanterns, where they were all drinking whiskey from great barrels all around. Nor did the other witches recognize them, for they had all been transformed into strange imp-like creatures, and he looked the same as the rest of them, and he saw no reason to reveal himself and went on drinking and singing with them and passed a lovely evening.

It was then that they heard a knock at the door of the cellar, and the lord of the castle came barging in with his men, and all of the witches magicked themselves away then, but Seamus knew not how, and he was changed back into his own appearance and arrested then, for he had no way to explain his situation, which was clearly the work of witchcraft.

His trial was swift, and he was set to hang, with many a spectator from the town gathered around, but then, among the laughter and the eager cries for his death, he heard the familiar voice of his old housekeeper, Madge, who cried out, "Seamus, are you so content to die without your cap and rue?" And at this, Seamus turned to one of the men and said that he was ready to die that day, but that he must, as his last request, be allowed to die with his cap and his twig of rue, which were, of course, granted him.

And then he spoke the charm as before, and flew into the air above the crowd, and flew all the way home, where he blessed and thanked the old witch Madge, his housekeeper, and allowed her to keep her strange witcheries and headstrong ways. And he kept her in his employment for the rest of their days, for they were quite good friends afterwards.

The Bent Needle
New World

Once, near Clayton, North Carolina, there lived an infamous conjure-man by the name of Dr. Duncan, who was believed by many to possess powers both to cure and to curse, to heal and to torment, depending on the circumstance.

Dr. Duncan was both loved and feared by the Black community in equal measure. He was sought after by folks who believed they had been spelled or bewitched, in which case he possessed the necessary countercharm to restore balance to one's body and soul. He could also remove mundane maladies, and it was believed that when he "drew" the ailment from whatever portion of the body it happened to be in, be it the back, the stomach, the foot, or what have you, it would come out of the body as a living toad, and would hop away.

But the fear of this conjure-man's craft was very real as well. They say that once, Dr. Duncan was paid a visit by a local woman who had suffered abuse at the hands of a neighbor for a very long time. For a fee, the conjure-man agreed to enact the curse that would bring her enemy low again. And it was done in this way, according to legend: he lit a candle before him, and heated a needle in its flame until its metal became soft and bendable, then he curled the thing round, sticking its point through its own eye. In the days that followed, the woman's tormentor began to stoop more and more as she walked, until her back curled up entirely, and she died so thoroughly bent, they say, that her head lay beside her feet.

The Wart Tree
England

Several generations ago, though not so many that it be in ancient times, there lived a young family with a boy child who was ever found playing in the muck and filth, running through creeks and fields, and generally always requiring a bath. He was especially fond of catching toads and carrying them around with him everywhere, pulling them out at school or at church so as to frighten anyone he could.

And it so happened that the child's hands became riddled with warts of an increasing number and size, which was appalling to his parents, but not surprising to anyone who knew of his wild behavior. The mother tried every remedy known to her, but none seemed capable of removing the warts from his fingers, until at last the family decided to consult a local charmer, called by some a healer and others a witch.

Now, this old woman asked the family to meet her near an old ash tree in the month of May at an appointed time, which they did, though they were perhaps a bit wary of seeking a witch's aid in a matter involving their child. The cunning woman told them not to worry, and comforted them, then produced from her shawl a little packet containing a line of pins. "Don't be afraid, child," said the old woman to the boy, who clutched at his mother's skirt. "This won't hurt much. I promise you."

She then took one of the pins between her fingers and stuck its dull end into the bark of the old ash tree firmly, so that it stayed there, embedded in its gnarled surface. She took the boy's hand then, and whispering a strange charm, pressed the wart on his index finger so that the pin in the tree went through it, piercing it. The boy flinched, for it did hurt some, but not as much as he thought. And so the witch continued, setting a new pin in the bark for each wart, then pressing it through while whispering her charms.

At the end of the ordeal, the boy was quite glad to be finished, and the woman was paid for her expertise. And though the parents were suspicious that they had been quite scammed by the cunning woman, the potency of her strange craft spoke for itself, for the boy's warts all shrank in the weeks that followed, shriveling until they were gone at last.

Years later, they say that the boy returned to his hometown as a young man to visit family, and he made his way to that old ash tree in the countryside overlooking the lush meadows and pastures that he remembered from his youth. The great tree was still there, standing sentinel over the fields. What's more, it was covered with pins stuck all over its bark, so many pins that he could not count them all if he tried, evidence that the witch was still at her work, even so many years later, for every pin stuck in that old ash tree signified one wart that she had removed from a client.

The Horseshoe
Scotland

It happened on Tiree, long ago, that a farmer had become quite frustrated at his loss of livestock. He kept his heifers in a byre made in the old way, out of wooden stakes woven with branches so as to make a kind of fence wall. Night after night, the stakes and branches would slide and fall, and his heifers would be injured by it, some even being strangled, caught in the collapsed branches. No reasoning could account for the collapse of the byre's structure, for it was soundly built, and none of the family nor any neighbor could make sense of it.

At last, suspecting witchcraft, the man consulted a local wise woman who was purported to be a witch herself, though of the helpful kind. These cunning women or charmer women would often be consulted in matters such as this, for they knew the secret mechanics of curses, and so could be trusted to identify the counter-charm to put a stop to such things.

Upon hearing of the farmer's troubles, the witch advised the man to take a horseshoe with three iron nails in it, and to hang it upon the byre where the heifers rested. In addition to this, she told him to take a silver coin and bury it below the threshold of the structure. Lastly, he was to take the hind quarter of one of the murdered animals and bury it to the West of his property, just beyond the fence line.

Having done all of this, the man found that his byre fell no more, and his heifers were quite safe, though he perhaps wondered about the owners of the property just to the West of his, and whether the wise woman's advice to bury the hindquarter on the edge of their property might mean that they were the witches who had cursed his byre in the first place. For such things do happen, whether out of jealousy or spite.

Churchyard Dirt
Wales

Long ago, in a village in Wales, there lived a man who was an infamous gambler. He owned a black rooster, a fearsome-looking thing, which he prized above all else, for he was an avid cock-fighting enthusiast, winning every match he ever undertook. The rumors about his suspiciously good fortune pointed to witchcraft and the black arts, though none could confirm it.

Another gambling man, having lost countless matches, and having impoverished himself over months, decided to take matters into his own hands and consult a nearby charmer to see if witchcraft was indeed at work, and if so, what could be done about it.

"Sorcery it is, certainly," said the charmer, "but what is it to you? Why do you waste your time fighting these poor birds against one another and throwing away your coin? To think, a grown man like yourself. Why not do something else, and let it be?"

"Because I am a gambler, ma'am, through and through," he replied, "and gambling is what I do best."

"Very well," said the charmer. "In order to dispel this craft, you will need to visit the local churchyard. Be sure to go at night, and let none see you. Take three handfuls of soil, and before the next cock-fight, scatter it about the fighting pit, and the charm will be broken."

"Must it be churchyard dirt? Why not any old dirt?"

"Ah," replied the old charmer. "His power comes from a spirit with whom he has made compact. But the sanctified ground has its own secrets, and has no love for a cheat."

And so the poor gambling man did as he was told. He set off just before midnight, when all of the town was asleep, and he made his way to the old churchyard, where the dead of the several hundred years were buried. The night air was cold, and the moonlight was barely bright enough to see his way along the path. Once or twice, as he was gathering handfuls of earth into his pouch, he could swear he heard footsteps or saw a dark figure in the corner of his eye, but he resolved not to think on this too much, and neither should we, dear reader, for the spirits of such places hold secret vigils of their own, and such matters are not for us to know.

The next morning, before the cock-fighting match was set to commence, the poor gambler secretly scattered the churchyard earth over the fighting pit. Just as the charmer had foretold, the gambler with the black cock finally lost a match, and the poor man, having borrowed as much as he could to place against him, was able to make all of his coin back.

As the black cock died, the pitiful thing stared directly into the poor gambler's eyes and cried out, then coughed up a little clod of soil. The man gave up gambling that very day, and he never attended another cock-fight for the rest of his life.

The Old Black Cats
New World

There once was a young girl who was hired into the service of two elderly ladies, both unmarried. Despite having no husbands or children to care for, the ladies kept a proper New England home, and the girl was tasked with the cooking, cleaning, shopping, and whatever else was required. Needless to say, she worked quite hard, and often quite late, and it was not unusual for her to still be at her work long after sundown.

Over time, she noticed that the behavior of the two old maids was, at times, quite strange. Most folk of a certain age take to bed at an early hour and rise early with the sun, but these two were always late to rise in the mornings. The girl frequently noticed that they were gone late in the evening, though she never saw them leave through the front door. What bothered her most, though, was the presence of two old black cats on these nights. They would appear in the strangest of places, and only at night, staring at her with their golden eyes, which gave her a chill, then departing together, side by side, walking down the old road to who knows where.

One Sunday afternoon, the girl was visiting her mother in a nearby town, and she could not help but tell her all of this strange business. Her mother, who was known among all local Black families to be a very accomplished conjure woman, sipped her tea, squinted her eyes knowingly, and said quite matter-of-factly, "They must be witches after all, then."

"Do you think so?" said the girl.

"There have been rumors about those two among the folk in town," replied her mother. "And signs that it may be true. But we can find out for sure." And with that, her mother explained to her the plan they would enact together, telling her what must be done in order to determine whether the two white women were witches or not.

Upon returning to her employers, the girl did as her mother instructed. She convinced the two women that she had injured herself while visiting family and would have her mother come and stay with them for a couple of nights, just until she regained her strength. The old women offered to treat her with their own remedies, made from herbs they grew in their own garden, but the girl refused, lest the lie be revealed.

When her mother arrived, she spent the day working at all the chores the girl would ordinarily tend to, busying herself long into the evening. Once the two old white women had retired to bed, the mother went to fetch the girl, and they both crept silently up the stairs, hiding just outside the bedroom door, so that they might watch through the keyhole and observe for themselves any witchery afoot.

The two women undressed themselves before the great hearth in the room, whispering as if unto an unseen stranger in the flames, then peeled off their own skin into two great heaps on the floor, revealing the very black cats that the girl had so often seen at night. The two creatures scampered up the chimney then, somehow untouched by the flames, and there was a sound as if a great wind had passed over the roof.

"Witches for sure," the girl's mother remarked with glee. "Now the fun begins, child."

But the girl was not thrilled by what she had seen, only afraid. "Shouldn't we be careful? Aren't witches dangerous?"

"Oh, yes. The bad ones, anyway. They can take the milk from your cows, the life from your land, and the vitality from your very bones. They can take everything there is. But only if you let them." And with that, her mother took a bit of salt and pepper from her pocket and sprinkled it on the inside of the skins left on the floor. "Now we wait," she said slyly.

When the two black cats returned down the chimney and tried to crawl back into the skins, they let out such terrible yowls that the girl had to put her hand over her mouth to keep from making a sound. Out they would jump, unable to assume their prior shape, then in they would climb again, trying repeatedly to enter the skins they had abandoned.

This went on for quite some time, and though the mother was amused, the girl was not. Her mother could not stay with her forever, she knew. What would become of her when the witches eventually discovered who had played such a trick on them? Eventually, the cats realized what was afoot and shook out the skins, scattering the salt and pepper across the floor.

"Who would do such a thing, do you think?" asked the one.

"None but some conjuror, having a laugh at our expense," said the other.

The girl's mother smiled, and the two crept off quietly, without making a sound, leaving the witches to their business. They did not speak a word until they were out the door and had shut it firmly behind them. What the girl's mother whispered to her then, none can say for certain, but it was the beginning of the girl's training in the conjuring arts her mother had mastered over many years, arts which had protected her from many monsters in her life—be they cruel employers, wicked sorcerous folk, or in this case, both at once.

After that night, the girl's mother returned to her own home, and the two witches seemed for the most part unharmed, though they did scratch themselves from time to time, as if a grain or two of the salt and pepper were still stuck under their skins. With her mother's guidance, the young girl became something of a charmer herself, and her tricks softened up the two old white women quite a bit in the years that followed, until eventually, they weren't so unpleasant to work for at all. Still, the girl always kept a good supply of salt and pepper, just in case.

The Kerrow Witch
Cornwall

It was near the village of Zennor that a hunter once injured a witch, albeit quite by accident—a grave mistake for which he suffered in the years to come. Witching folk are like faerie folk in that way, or so they say; though human and capable of forgiveness, their memory is long, and their grudges run deep.

It was the custom of a certain young lord to go hunting near Kerrow, and each morning, beside a certain pond, he spied a rather large hare that would quickly fly through the grass, escaping into a drain pipe that emptied into the pool. The creature's persistent escape vexed him for days until he decided to embark one morning with a small hunting party to aid him.

The young lord explained to the men that the hare was quite fast and quite clever, and he conveyed how it escaped him by jumping into the drain pipe.

"My lord," said one of his men, "that pipe runs to a nearby house, and the woman who lives there is suspected of all manner of witchcraft, both good and ill. It would be wise to let the creature be, lest we anger the witch by harming her servant."

"Nonsense," said the young lord with a chuckle, for he firmly believed, as young heirs often do, that his youth and his wealth entitled him to a bit of fun where he could find it.

Once again, he spied the hare sitting beside the pool, and he fired three shots. The first flew too low, hitting the still waters of the pool, and causing a ripple to spread across its surface. The second flew too high, scattering bark from a nearby oak tree. The third shot, which landed just as the hare bolted into the drain pipe, surely grazed its ear, but the creature had disappeared into the darkness once more, albeit with a painful wound, though not a lethal one.

"Surely the thing is injured enough to catch it," said the young lord, who then insisted that the men accompany him to the nearby house that fed the drain. The men reluctantly obeyed, fearing the displeasure of the young man more than the displeasure of the witch, which was, in the end, an unfortunate choice indeed.

When the company arrived at the house and knocked upon the door, there was no answer, but the young lord insisted that it was perfectly acceptable to enter nonetheless. There, in the middle of the room, sat an elderly woman with long, flowing gray hair and a scornful expression on her face. The side of her head was matted with fresh blood, which was running down her arm as she held her hand to her head. The look she gave the men turned their blood cold, for without speaking a word, it conveyed a rage as hot as the fires of hell itself. A great black cat, larger than any housecat the men had ever seen, then leapt down from a shelf, standing between them and the woman, baring its teeth. Its eyes glowed like hot coals, they say, and the men were gripped by a sense of dread they could not explain. They fled the house, never to return.

The witch survived her injury and lived long afterwards, it is said, as evidenced by the fate of that wayward hunting party. They say the wealth of the young lord's family dwindled in the years to come, that they could find success in none of their endeavors, until their great house came at last to ruin. And the men who accompanied him on the hunt could catch no game from that day forward, for every shot they fired would always miss its target.

Elf-Bolts
Scotland

Perhaps the most famous of all the accused Scottish witches during the dark times of the witch-hunts was Isobel Gowdie of Auldearn, who came forward of her own volition to confess to witchcraft in 1662, without arrest or torture. In her lengthy confessions, Gowdie references several known elements of witch lore at the time, including charms for flying through the air, meetings with the Devil, dining with faery spirits who live under the earth, and cursing neighbors.

One of the more interesting items mentioned by Isobel Gowdie is the "elf-bolt," which was used to inflict harm upon others by flinging it at them while traveling in spirit form.

The "elf-bolt" was so-called, according to her, because it was sharpened to a point by "elf boys." After each bolt was made by the Devil, it was given over to the elves to trim to a very sharp point using a kind of needle, after which, the Devil would hand them over to his witches, saying:

> "Shoot these in my name,
> And they sall not goe heall hame."

According to Gowdie, the witches would shoot the elf-bolts by flicking them from their thumbnails, an act that seems almost reminiscent of a children's game with stones or marbles. As they flicked the bolts, the witches would say:

> "I shoot yon man in the devillis name,
> He sall nott win heall hame!
> And this salbe alswa trw,
> Thair sall not be an bitt of him on liew."

These elf-bolts, of course, are also known throughout Scotland and Ireland, and indeed throughout the world, as arrowheads, the remnants of weapons used by prehistoric indigenous tribes for thousands of years. In Scotland, these arrowheads are most frequently found around "faery hills," or ancient burial mounds. Even in the days of Gowdie, these "bolts" were kept as amulets and charms by those with a love of superstition, and also by those with an interest in charming and witchery.

The accused witch Catherine Ross was believed, in the course of her trials, to have set up clay figures of her intended victims—the clay corpse, or corp creadha, a type of poppet—in order to throw "elf bolts" at them, these bolts again being prehistoric arrowheads found throughout rural places.

Some accused of witchcraft were believed to have offered their services combating, preventing, or mitigating the effects of "elf arrows" cast upon persons in their community. Bartie Paterson was a skilly man or cunning man accused of preventing harm to cattle by means of the following spoken charm:

> *I charme thee for arrow-schot,*
> *For dor-schot, for wondo-schot,*
> *For ey-schot, for tung-schot,*
> *For lever-schot, for lung-schot,*
> *For hert-schot, all the maist,*
> *In the name of the Father, the Sone,*
> *And the Haly Ghaist.*
> *To wend out of fleisch and bane,*
> *Into stek and stane,*
> *In the name of the Father, the Sone,*
> *And the Haly Ghaist. Amen.*

This charm appears throughout Scottish witching lore during this time period, and so it appears to be an authentic charm of many variations. The invocation of the trinity here would alone have been appalling to witch-hunters, as opposed as they were to the ritualistic elements of Catholicism.

Other accounts of folklore connected to these fairy arrows are numerous. Some say that the elves would steal away a human to do their bidding, for the bolts must be thrown by human hands, and so the task of afflicting their victims would be completed by a kidnapped person who was for some reason selected to join their dark company. But conversely, the elf-bolt worn about the neck was believed to be a potent talisman against harm, especially against dark witchcraft and the workings of the faery folk. And any water in which it was dipped was believed to be blessed and made suitable for workings of healing and protection.

The Devil's Den
Isle of Man

Long ago, near the foot of the great hill of South Barrule, there was once believed to have been a deep chasm in the earth, a pit that folk once called *The Devil's Den*. It was a place thought to be under the power of the witching folk, and used by them for dark purposes.

Some said that human voices could be heard within, crying out in misery. It has been said, too, that there was once an old man passing by the spot, who he saw what appeared to be a great serpent or dragon with glowing eyes and wings. It was so large, according to the account, that its shadow blotted out the sun and made the entire area around as dark as night. It stretched its wings, they say, then descended and flew into the pit.

But by most accounts, the Devil's Den was used in ancient times by the witches of old. It was a place of punishment and imprisonment, for when one offended the witching folk of the ancient island, they could trap the victim in the pit for as long as they pleased. And it is said that an ancient prince is still down there, at the bottom of that dark place, having offended the sorcerous people of the island hundreds of years ago, a crime for which he is punished with both imprisonment and immortality, living forever in that darkness to this very day, and for the rest of time.

A Silver Bullet
New World

Once, in the rolling green hills of Lincoln County, North Carolina, there lived a hunter who was making his way through the woods in search of game. He was well-known for being an excellent shot with his gun, and he would usually come home with something or other that could be cleaned and prepared for his family's dinner that evening.

As he wandered through the trees, he spied a turkey of enormous size, fat and round, and thinking that this would make a fine supper indeed, he aimed his gun and took his shot. At this, the turkey merely shook its feathers, looking him squarely in the eyes, unphased. He shot again, and again, and at each instance, the bird merely shook its feathers and stared. No matter how many times he fired his gun at the thing, it was unharmed and unafraid, and so eventually, the man left, convinced there must be something wrong with his gun or with his own eyes.

This, however, was not the case. For his gun fired well at any other target, and his eye did not fail him except in shooting the wild turkey. He told his neighbor what had happened, and that neighbor informed him that nearby, just a short walk from the place where he was hunting, lived a notorious witch-man, who was "famous all over the county as a witch of witches," and that this creature was in fact the old witch-man himself, taken into animal form, as was his custom. He told him that the only way to take down such a creature was with a silver bullet.

And so the hunter melted down some silver he possessed and fashioned himself a bullet made of its metal, and he returned to the spot where he had previously encountered the wild turkey, and there it was again before him, standing as proudly as ever, and unafraid. He then took out his silver bullet from his jacket pocket, and the thing glinted in the sun so that the turkey could see what it was, and it was then that the creature bolted away with such speed that he could not see where it went. And the hunter never did see the witch-bird again after that day.

Cats' Paws
Scotland

Many generations ago, in what was a very different world than this one, there lived in a small village a young couple who were ever so eager to begin a family of their own. They had long hoped for a child, and when at last the woman gave birth to a boy, they were overjoyed.

It was not long after, however, that the babe took ill. It refused to nurse, crying at all hours. The midwife tried every remedy available to her, until at last she had exhausted her knowledge and was forced to tell the young couple that their beloved child was not long for this world.

News spread of the poor child's fate, for gossip moved through the village faster than fish in the sea. Neighbors and acquaintances stopped by to bring comfort, food, and prayers, though none of this brought relief to the young parents, who looked more and more gaunt and haggard from lack of sleep and from long hours of crying at the fate of their child.

At last, a cunning woman, whom some in the village called a witch, paid a visit to the couple. Despite the rumors about the old woman, the young parents welcomed her into their home, offering her what little they had in the way of refreshment. "I'll see the child myself this day," the cunning woman said abruptly, interrupting their small talk. "If the babe is as ill as they say, we've no time to waste on polite nonsense."

The couple shared a nervous look between them, but ultimately led the witch to the child's cradle. After all, with no other options left to them, what else were they to do? The well-known herbal remedies had failed them. Perhaps the old cunning arts could save their child's life.

The old woman bent over the babe in its cradle and placed one hand upon its forehead, gazing intently into its eyes. She muttered something under her breath, strange words that the parents could not quite discern.

"Well," interrupted the mother, "Do you believe you can cure it?"

"No," said the cunning woman. "There be no cure. This sickness has no remedy. No medicines will deter it from its course."

"Then there is no hope," said the father, solemnly.

"That's not what I said," said the witch. "The sickness cannot be cured, but it can be taken, and it can be given."

The young parents looked baffled.

"Do as I say," continued the witch, "and your child will be well again. Gather for me a candle, a large bowl of clean water, a black cat, and some thread as red as blood."

The parents could not but acquiesce, of course, and brought to the old woman the ingredients she needed to work the charm: a candle, a bowl of clean water, a spool of red thread, and a black cat.

First, the witch closed the curtains, leaving the room very dark indeed. Then, she lit the candle, muttering some other strange words as she did so. With the bowl of water on the table before her, she picked up the cat then, and dipped its two front paws into the bowl of water, at which the confused thing growled and hissed briefly, then retreated to clean itself in the corner.

The old woman dipped her hands into the bowl of water, and she began stroking the child's head, muttering her incantations in a low voice. She cut a length of the red thread, soaked it in the water, then tied it around the babe's neck as a kind of necklace. It was what the witch did next, however, that most frightened the young couple.

The witch began gasping for air as if her throat had become very narrow, a raspy, noisome sound emerging from her as if from one at death's door. She gasped long and hard, then exhaled in a loud, moaning sigh, with such volume that the candle flame began to flicker. Her loud breathing continued on for quite a while, and it became louder and louder each time as the husband and wife watched on, wide-eyed, their hands held tightly in fear.

The witch at last fell still then, and when she opened her eyes, she did not look well at all. Her eyes were bloodshot, and her skin slightly blue. Her breathing was haggard and strained. The child, on the other hand, let out a sharp cry, its first true cry since taking ill, and its color was pink and rosy, and its cheeks were warm with life.

"You took his illness into yourself!" cried out the mother, who lifted her babe in her arms, kissing him and hugging him tight.

"For now," said the witch in a tired voice, making her way to the door. "Live well, child," she said with a smile, then shut the door behind her.

People in the village said that the child grew healthy and happy after that day, though the same could not be said of all, for the witch's landlord, who was known to be a cruel and crooked man, fell deathly ill soon after and passed from this life. Quite mysteriously, or perhaps not so mysteriously at all, it was around this same time that the witch regained her own health.

The Buried Sheaf
Ireland

One of the more interesting curses of Irish witchcraft was supposedly utilized as recently as the late 1800s near the village of Louth. It is known as "burying the sheaf," and it is a distinct form of the well-known witch's poppet, which was often employed in Scotland via a human likeness made of clay, but was, in Ireland, fashioned using wheat. By old accounts, this wheat doll was made carefully, almost lovingly, and even featured a heart made of plaited straw at its chest.

Like other witches' poppets, the wheat doll was often (though not always) utilized in order to punish and injure the enemy. The thing would be stuck through with various pins, often placed at the joints. It would then be buried, much like a mock-funeral, while curses were spoken aloud, often a kind of dark eulogy that was said to include the phrase "in the name of the Devil."

If the witch intended a quick death for the victim, the doll would be buried in ground that was moist and wet and inclined to rot, for this would hasten the decay of the wheat doll and speed death along. If the death was meant to be slow and languishing and more agonizing for the victim, it would be buried in very dry soil, where the process of decomposition would take a long while, a crueler fate for certain.

The Witch's Mill
New World

A great many years ago, somewhere in the Catskill Mountains of New York, there lived a miller and wife who were much troubled. The mill that they owned, which was set up on a bit of rock in the middle of a river, would not turn, and no cause could be found. After trying every solution, the miller and his wife reasoned that the mill itself must be witched.

Eventually, it was decided that they would hire a witching man, a charmer who could undo curses, to bring the old mill back to operation. And the witching man inspected the mill himself, and he confirmed that it was indeed cursed, and he offered them a means of dispelling the witchery at work. "Find me a man who will not speak a word," he said to them. "For he must be able to be silent and not cry out, no matter how afraid he is, and he must be willing to do all that I ask of him."

This seemed an impossible task to the couple, but after some searching, they were able to find an old farmer who was quite down on his luck, and was very willing to do what they asked for a small fee. And so they brought him to the witching man, just as asked.

The instructions he gave the old farmer were precise, and were to be followed to the latter. The witching man gave him a piece of paper with strange words and shapes scrawled on it, and he told him that he must fasten it to the millstone, but could speak no word until the task was complete. Nor could he shout, or sigh, or hum, or make any sound at all. Once the paper was fixed in place, then and only then, he was to shout as loud as he could, and this would turn back the bewitchment set upon the mill.

So the old man began to make his way, for it was already late in the day, and the sun was going down over the mountains. He walked to the little boat at the edge of the water and boarded it with his lantern in hand, for it was necessary to take a boat in order to reach the old mill, it being a short drift downstream and set in the middle of the current. The water was still and quiet, and the wind had died, and before long, darkness had fallen over the mountains, and the woods all around were drenched in shadow, and the water beneath the little boat was black as onyx. The only light upon the river was from the small lantern on the boat.

It was then that the man felt something brush against his side, as if someone were seated beside him on the vessel. He remembered the words of the witching man, though, and did not cry out, pretending not to notice the sensation. He pushed the boat to shore, and just as he was it up by means of a tree, he felt someone blow into his ear, but again, he remembered the words of the witching man, and he did not cry out.

He ran to the entrance of the old mill, then, and just as he was almost to the door, he felt someone grab him about the neck and shoulders, as if trying to hold him back. He pushed his way through, staying silent the whole time, and rushed to the old millstone and fastened the enchanted paper to it. And at this, he yelled as loud as he could, just as he had been instructed, and the mill immediately began to turn again. He felt no invisible guests on his ride home, and all seemed as it should be, and the old man was glad to be done with the whole thing.

It was not long after, however, that the miller's wife took ill with a strange sickness, the likes of which the family had never seen before. She seemed to be weak and feeble without explanation, and she was wasting away day by day. And so the miller sent his son to the witching man once more, to tell him of what was happening, for surely some new witchery must be the cause.

When the miller's son arrived at the witching man's house and explained what was happening to his mother, the man's face grew cold as ice.

"Of course she's taken ill," he said to the boy. "She was the witch who cursed the millstone, and all of her dark magic has been turned back against her."

The Witch's Helper
England

Once, long ago, there lived a very poor family with two young daughters. Hard times had fallen upon their little farm, and with another winter, they knew that they would surely be in hunger's grasp. In those times, it was customary for poor families to send their girls into the service of wealthier households, where they could earn wages for their family in return for cleaning, cooking, and errands. And with the threat of starvation upon them, the family knew at last that this was their only option.

It was decided, then, that the first daughter would go off down the road, searching for a great house that would offer her a servant's role. Though the girl did not wish to become a servant, but wanted only to play and to be young and free as all children do, she did not wish to see her family starve. And so she set off on her journey, with her love for her family in her heart, lending her courage as she went.

The girl traveled through a deep, dark wood, thick with briar that snagged at her clothes. But she carried on until she came to a little clearing in the trees where stood a great stone oven, roaring away as it baked.

"Please, child," said the oven, "Won't you take these loaves from my belly? I've been baking them for seven long years, and they'll burn if they're left in any longer."

"Let me help," said the girl, who then removed every loaf carefully and set them neatly upon a nearby stone table. And having finished helping, she continued on her way.

The girl proceeded through the dark wood further on, briars and thorns and all, until she came to another clearing in the trees, and in the middle of this clearing stood a cow.

"Please, child," said the cow, "Won't you milk me? I have been waiting for seven long years, and my udders are so terribly full they may burst."

"Let me help," said the girl, who quickly grabbed a nearby pail and milked the cow until it was filled to the brim. And having finished helping, she continued on her way.

The girl pushed even further through the dark wood, and at last, she came to another clearing in the trees, and in the middle of this clearing was a great apple tree.

"Please, child," said the tree, "Won't you pick my apples? It's been seven long years I've waited, and the weight of them is sure to split me in two."

"Let me help," said the girl, who climbed up the tree as nimbly as you please and made quick work of the task, leaving a great pile of apples on the grass nearby. And having finished helping, she continued on her way.

The girl pressed on through the dark and terrible wood, keeping the love of her family in her mind and in her heart, for she was quite afraid. At long last, though, she came to another clearing in the trees, and in the middle of this clearing stood a handsome estate. Remembering her mission, the girl knocked upon the door to ask if she might serve the owners of the home.

It was not a lord or lady who answered the door, however, but a witch. Now, ordinarily, witchcraft is not considered the most lucrative of professions, and a witch's house would not make for an ideal posting for any servant, but the girl remembered her family's plight, and having come so far, she thought she might as well inquire.

"Good woman," said the girl, "Might you need a servant in your fine home? I'll work very hard, and I would be ever so grateful for fair wages. My family has fallen on such hard times."

The witch eyed the girl from her head down to her feet, then cracked the faintest smile. "We have a deal, then, girl. It's been seven years since my last servant left, and there is much work piled up around here."

And so the girl stayed in the witch's employ for a good long while, tending her oven and her cow and her apple tree, and doing the cleaning and the cooking and many other things besides. The witch paid her fairly for her labor, and though she said little to the girl, the two got on amicably in their own way.

One day, while the witch was away from the house on some important business to do with her witchcraft, the girl noticed something shining in the fireplace soot, and upon closer inspection, found a great pile of gold coins just beneath the ashes. *To steal from a witch is a grave thing, indeed*, she thought, but the fear of her family's hunger tugged at her heart, and so she took the gold and fled the house to head back to her own home. On her way out the door, however, she saw the witch approaching, and fled hastily. The witch followed after at her own slow pace.

The girl came once more to the little clearing with the apple tree. "Oh, tree! Please hide me. I fear I've angered the witch, and she will surely harm me if she finds me!" And so the girl climbed into the tree's great branches and hid as the witch approached.

"Good tree," said the witch, "Have you seen a servant girl?"

"No, Mother," said the tree, "No servant girl have I seen this day."

The witch scratched her chin and narrowed her eyes, and went on her way.

The girl fled the tree then, and she came once more to the little clearing with the cow. "Oh, cow! Please hide me. I fear I've angered the witch, and she will surely harm me if she finds me!" And so the girl hid behind the cow as the witch approached.

"Good cow," said the witch, "Have you seen a servant girl?"

"No, Mother," said the cow, "No servant girl have I seen this day."

The witch scratched her chin and narrowed her eyes, and went on her way.

The girl fled from behind the cow then, and she came once more to the little clearing with the oven. "Oh, oven! Please hide me. I fear I've angered the witch, and she will surely harm me if she finds me!" And so the girl hid inside the oven as the witch approached.

"Good oven," said the witch, "Have you seen a servant girl?"

"No, Mother," said the oven, "No servant girl have I seen this day."

The witch took out her pipe then and lit it, and took a very long puff. "Well, then," she said at last with a smile, "I suppose the servant girl is quite gone now, and with so much gold no less. And in return for all she has done, my curse be this: *May she never serve in another house for the rest of her days.*" And with that, the witch returned home.

When the girl rejoined her family, they were overjoyed to see her, but money does strange things to folks, and though this gold was enough to keep them comfortable and happy for the rest of their lives, they desired more. At last, they conspired to send the second daughter to the witch's house and repeat the feat a second time so that they could be twice as wealthy. The second daughter scowled and huffed at the idea, for she was a spiteful creature, but she went on with it nonetheless.

Walking the same path through the dark woods, the second daughter came upon the oven, the cow, and the apple tree, just as the first one did, and even though it had only been days and not years since they were tended, which would have been short work indeed, she refused to help any of them at all. "What care I for your troubles? I've a fortune to win," she said to each one, coldly.

Eventually, the second daughter knocked upon the door of the witch's estate, just as the first one did, and sure enough, the witch agreed to employ her. But this girl's work was only ever half-hearted, and at the end of each day, as she took her coin from the witch in fair payment, she sneered and huffed, expecting her own great pile of gold.

A day came when the witch needed to travel on the road on some important business of witchcraft yet again, and just as before, the second daughter spied the glittering gold in the fireplace. Without a second thought, she greedily gathered it all up in a great bundle and made off into the wood. It was not long down the path, however, before she spied the witch coming behind her.

The second daughter came once more to the clearing with the apple tree. "Hide me quickly, fool!" demanded the girl. "The witch comes for me!"

"Why should I care for your troubles?" replied the tree. And so the girl had no choice but to press on, fleeing the witch's wrath, which was even closer than before.

She came next to the little clearing with the cow. "Hide me quickly, fool cow!" demanded the girl. "The witch comes for me!"

"Why should I care for your troubles?" replied the cow. And so the girl had no choice but to press on, running as quickly as she could now, for the witch was closer still.

She came at last to the little clearing with the oven. Realizing this was her last chance to hide, she attempted a sweeter tone with this one. "Please, dear oven!" cried the girl, "Won't you hide me in your belly?"

"I would help you," replied the oven, "But I am full of burned and bitter bread that you did not take out in time, and there is no room for you at all."

"Damned fool!" screeched the girl, who hastily tossed all the burned bread onto the ground and climbed inside to hide from the witch, who arrived not a moment later.

"Good oven," said the witch with a smile, eyeing the loaves of burned bread scattered about, "Have you seen a servant girl?"

"Indeed I have, Mother," replied the oven, "She's here, in my very belly. A servant she is, and a servant she'll be forevermore, no matter how much gold she has."

And at this, the witch grabbed the girl up by the ankle and wrested her from the oven, lifting her up by her foot, and shaking loose every last bit of gold. "What a good worker you are, girl, to finally get around to cleaning this poor oven. In return for all you've done, my blessing on your head be this: *may you always be employed in service, for the rest of your long days.*"

When the second daughter returned home and told her parents all that had transpired, they were greatly vexed. And even greater was their vexation upon realizing that their first daughter had left with the greater share of the gold, presumably to live her own life elsewhere, leaving her scheming family to their own devices.

A Corpse of Clay
Scotland

It was on cold, dark evenings that Maclain Ghiarr of the Isle of Mull would ride horseback, surveying the hillsides for cattle that he might steal, as was his custom. Raiding was a dangerous matter indeed, but doubly so for Maclain, for the Isle of Mull has always been famous for its witches, and during the age of the highland clans, practitioners of the art would gather at night in remote places and crumbling ruins in the countryside in order to conduct their craft. On occasion, Maclain could swear he saw strange lights flickering in the old ruins of the Pennygown Kirkyard, but he dared not approach, for the graves there were ancient, and who knows what business the spirits have in such old places in the dark of the night.

Maclain continued his nightly raiding for many years, and over that time, he stole so many cattle from a neighboring chief that he was pronounced the clan's sworn enemy. The chief swore that he would kill the criminal himself with his own two hands, should he ever show himself in his presence. Maclain, of course, being a raider, cared not, and continued his business of theft and lawlessness without so much as a flicker of remorse.

As the next few weeks passed on, though, strange rumors began to circulate around the Isle of Mull. The chief who had pronounced Maclain his mortal enemy had become the target of the island's witches, who were angry with him over some unknown slight, and with each passing day, the chief became weaker and frailer, falling into the throws of strange pains and fits, such that no healer could cure or even comfort him. Many, of course, wondered what the chief would have done or said to anger the witches so, but he would not say, and so even we, dear reader, are left only to imagine. Perhaps he had broken some promise, or worse, broken a heart. Perhaps he had given insult quite by accident. Who can say?

In any case, the chief at last became gravely ill, and finally, one fateful night, in the midst of his screams and fits, the healers finally threw up their hands and declared that the man was on death's door and would surely be a corpse by morning.

But it was on this very night that Maclain, on one of his routine nightly rides, spied again the strange lights in the old Pennygown Kirkyard, and rather than pass by this time, found himself possessed of a desire to see for himself at last what business was going on in the old chapel ruins, among its crumbling walls and crooked gravestones.

Maclain tied his horse nearby, and approached quietly so as to watch unseen from behind one broken wall of the old chapel ruins, and what he saw within turned his blood cold. There, gathered about a small fire in the middle of the old chapel, stood a number of witches, speaking strange words and contorting themselves in a kind of dance. In the midst of the throng stood one witch nearest the fire, and in her hands, she held what appeared to be a clay doll fashioned in the likeness of the tormented chief. Its body was stuck all over with many pins, each one corresponding to one of the crippling pains that afflicted their victim.

Another witch approached the one with the clay poppet to hand her one final pin, much longer than the others, and just as the witch held it over the doll's heart, Maclain ran shouting into their midst to interrupt them, waving his sword and scattering the witches into the surrounding darkness. He gathered up the corp creadha, or clay body, from the ground, and he rode until he reached the home of the cursed chief.

After a great deal of convincing, he was finally allowed inside, and there lay the chief on his deathbed, his breath ragged and tortured, his skin pale as a corpse. He showed the man the little poppet he had stolen from the witches, and began removing the pins stuck in its clay flesh. As he pulled the first pin, the man let out a little sigh. As he pulled the second pin, the color returned to his cheeks. As he pulled the third pin, the man began to breathe easier. At last, once all of the pins were removed, the chief sat up in his bed and pronounced that Maclain Ghiarr, despite all of his crimes, was forgiven, and would come to no harm in his home.

One would like to say that Maclain retired from his raiding and criminal ways after that, but this would be untrue. As is often the case, the man was who he was, in the end, a raider and a scoundrel for certain, but perhaps even the wicked are capable of a moment of kindness, now and then.

The Counting Curse
Wales

It happened once near the village of Henllan that a famous conjuror was traveling, and having grown quite road-weary, he decided to stop at a pub for food and rest. In those days, the charmers of the countryside were well-known, and most folk were duly careful not to give offense to them, for though many were benevolent, one could never be sure what might happen if they were angered.

This conjuror, whose name was Dick Spot, ordered from the servant girl a plate of bread and cheese and a mug of ale to wash it down, for he was quite parched and famished from the road and much in need of refreshment. After he had eaten and drunk his fill, the servant girl charged him tenpence for it all, which was, in those days, outrageously high. Despite his protests, the girl insisted that he pay the hefty sum, and one cannot be sure if perhaps she charged him more than was custom, meaning to pocket the difference, thinking him some ordinary fool.

In any case, old Dick paid the tenpence, but before leaving the pub, he took out a little piece of paper from his pocket, and on this paper, he scrawled strange words and signs of enchantment, and he folded it neatly into a small square and tucked it within a large crack in a wooden table and left, smiling to himself.

It was later that evening that the strange events began. The owners of the pub, a man and his wife who kept their home upstairs on the second floor, were awoken from their sleep to the sounds of shouting. On coming down, they found the servant girl, the one who had overcharged the conjuror that very day, stomping her feet and dancing in the dead of night, shouting over and over again the words:

Six and four are ten!
Count it over again!

Though they tried to shake her from her trance, nothing could help, and the girl seemed to be compelled against her will to continue on.

Eventually, the wife tried to put her hand over the girl's mouth, if only to have a moment of peace from the endless repetition, but just as she did so, she lost control of her own body as well, as if the charm had become contagious in nature, spreading from one host to another. Almost immediately, she began to stomp her feet and dance, shouting:

Six and four are ten!
Count it over again!

This went on for some time until the husband tried to grab both of the women to hold their legs, if only to get them to stop their stomping and dancing for but a moment. The charm spread to him too, of course, and so he stood up straight against his own will and began dancing with them, shouting:

Six and four are ten!
Count it over again!

When the neighbors heard this riotous yelling and stomping, they eventually came over to see for themselves what was the matter, and knowing a bit more about the witching ways than their neighbors, they immediately went to visit the conjuror Dick Spot, who had taken a room at an inn nearby.

When they arrived, Dick was not asleep, but was watching through the window, laughing. He had expected someone to come visit him, of course, to ask how the curse could be removed. He then told the neighbors where the curse-note was hidden, and that they should remove it and burn it, and the spell would be lifted.

And just so, as soon as the note was burned, the couple and the servant girl regained control of themselves, and old Dick Spot left the next day on his way to Llanrwst. And perhaps, if they were wise, that pub was afterwards more hospitable to road-weary customers.

The Black Calf
New World

Once, there lived a young man in the rural farming country of New York. All of this happened long ago, so long ago that few today remember. Having fallen on hard times, he was forced to rent a room from a local, well-to-do widow and her daughter. Though they were kind and hospitable, the mother and daughter were quite strange in their ways, and many in the county suspected the pair of witchcraft. It was even said that the two of them would fly from the roof on certain nights of the year, only to return at break of day.

At first, the young man gave no thought to the rumors, but over time, he began to notice strange things in the house. The kitchen cabinets were stocked with strange ingredients— roots and powders that were neither medicinal nor culinary in nature. Above the doorways and across the porch of the old house were hung old brooms, horseshoes, bells, and holed stones. Strangest of all, on certain nights, he could hear creaking and scuffling on the rooftop, which vexed him terribly, for his room was in the attic of the old house, and these noises, which came always at midnight, would wake him from his sleep.

Eventually, the young man decided to see for himself what transpired on these nights, and so he waited night after night and watched through the keyhole of his bedroom door, which stood just opposite the stairs leading to his landlady's chamber. After weeks of waiting, his efforts were finally fruitful, for he saw the mother and daughter dressed all in black, walking silently by candlelight up the stairs to the old woman's bedroom.

He followed them quietly, staying several paces behind so as not to make a sound. Inside the old woman's bedroom, the two lit the small fireplace. The old woman produced from her shawl a jar, and having opened it, the two began to take gobs of grease from it with their fingertips, rubbing it all over themselves: across their necks, their foreheads, their arms, their legs, even the soles of their feet. At last, once they were sufficiently anointed, the two began to chant the words:

Over thick and over thin,
Away and away we go again.

No sooner were the words spoken than the two were transformed into a mass of black smoke, which churned and swirled and made its way through the fireplace and up the chimney, presumably onto the roof of the house.

Bearing witness to this sight should have been enough for the young tenant, but having been bitten by the bug of curiosity, he was possessed by a burning desire to know what the pair got up to on that rooftop. And so he proceeded to anoint himself with the grease as well, and to pronounce the magic words himself, at which he was immediately whisked up through the chimney.

He landed on the edge of the roof, where he saw the mother and daughter greet a little herd of black calves on another segment of the rooftop. Each mounted a black calf and spoke the words again, this time into the little calves' ears:

*Over thick and over thin,
Away and away we go again.*

No sooner was the charm spoken than the little black calves bore them up into the air, and astride their witch-steeds, the mother and daughter flew away into the black and windy night.

Well, having come this far already, the young man determined that it made no sense to stop now. And so he proceeded to mount one of the black calves himself. He leaned over to speak the magic words into the creature's ear, and the very next moment, he found himself riding the black calf through the night air, across great fields of farmland, until he came to the edge of a dark wood.

The black calf flew low then, weaving between the great trunks of aging trees, its hooves occasionally snapping a branch or scuffing against a bit of bark. The woods were so dense and dark that the young man could scarcely see anything at all, but the black calf seemed to know instinctively where it was headed.

Eventually, the calf landed on the edge of a little clearing in the woods, and the young man hid behind a large oak tree in order to watch what transpired there. The mother and daughter seemed to warmly greet a number of other witches, women and men of all ages and appearances, and at last, after the greetings were done, they proceeded to sing and dance in a ring around a central fire.

This lasted all night long. When the edge of the night sky began to turn blue with the coming of the dawn, the witches all mounted their animals once more—not only black calves, as the mother and daughter had ridden, but pigs, goats, donkeys, and all manner of creatures—and on their steeds, flew away through the wood to return to their homes.

When the last of the witches had departed, the young man mounted his black calf again, and just like the others, he was carried out through the dark wood once more and up into the blue-black sky, headed back in the direction of the little house. He realized then that he had not spoken a single word of thanks to the little black calf for all of this heavy lifting, and he felt that he should, out of politeness, express his gratitude to the creature.

"You do well, little calf," he said into the creature's ear, but at once, the thing began to flounder in the air and lose its balance, and then the two began falling, and while the little black calf landed safely on its hooves just on the edge of the wood, the young man was thrown violently into the branches of a great and twisted tree, bruising and scraping him badly on his way down. Sore and injured, the young man was forced to go the rest of the way on foot, which was no easy matter.

When he arrived at the old house, he was greeted by the mother-witch and daughter-witch, who were greatly concerned at the state of him. They helped to dress his wounds and fixed him a hot tea with whiskey, and he proceeded to tell them all that he had witnessed and how he had been injured that night. In gratitude for the kindness they had shown him, he promised not to tell a single soul.

The old woman stared at him then with a look that could have curdled milk, and he could not be sure of what she might do next. She was old, of course, but a witch nonetheless, and he was very weak. If she flew into a rage, he had no means of escape with his current injuries.

The younger witch who was her daughter could not keep a straight face, however, and broke into an impish grin, followed by a giggle.

At last, the old witch spoke. "Fool boy. Had you asked, I might have taught you better. One never speaks to a witch-steed in flight, lest the spell be broken."

The Witch's Sow
Cornwall

The witch known as Old Betty, who once lived in the village of St. Buryan, was quite famous for holding a very long grudge, even in matters so petty and trivial as to be forgotten by most folk. The story of her sow, and of how she came to acquire it, is an interesting one, indeed.

One day, a man named Tom, who was in truth a cousin of Old Betty's, was traveling from Penzance where he had bought a fine young pig at the market, with plans to fatten her up over the season so that she might be plump for a Christmas feast. It was on his way back home when Old Betty came up strolling behind him, shouting for him to stop.

"I placed my own offer for that sow, and you outbid me, Tom," said the witch.

"And I paid for her fairly. I've done nothing wrong," he replied.

"You will sell her to me for the price I offered," said Old Betty, "or misery will be thy very name."

Defiant, Tom refused the deal, saying, "I'll keep what I've bought at a fair price."

"And you'll soon take any price, any price at all," said the witch, "anything to be rid of that which you have taken from me today."

Tom walked away from the old woman then, but she continued shouting curses upon his head, shaking her finger at him and gesturing, her face twisted in bitter anger. Having known Betty all his life, he was perhaps used to her sour disposition, and he could not imagine that his own cousin would lay a terrible curse upon him in earnest.

He was, of course, wrong in his assumption. For the pig could not be penned, and it could not be fattened. No matter how securely he fixed the fence and the gate, the creature would escape and travel for miles, eventually destroying something on a neighbor's property that was expensive to replace. Nor would it eat as any healthy pig should, but instead grew leaner and leaner, shrinking as the weeks went on, until the thing was costing him more in damages each day than it could ever make up for, useless as it was for eating or for breeding.

Old Betty paid a visit to his farm on one particularly difficult day for Tom, who had spent the morning chasing down the creature after it destroyed most of a neighbor's garden, causing a loss that Tom himself would have to pay to replace.

"Once again, I'll offer to take that pig off your hands, you fool," said Old Betty. "Though since it's half the size now, I'll only pay half as much as before."

Tom was enraged. "I'll sell the sow at any price, no matter how cheap, before I allow you to have her," he said to the witch.

"We'll see," said Old Betty with a smile.

As days went on, Tom indeed found that he could not afford to keep the animal any longer and must be rid of it at once, and so he made his way to Penzance once more in order to sell it at the market, no matter how little it was worth. It was on the road that the pig began acting strangely, though, and just as they were about to cross a bridge, a strange-looking hare appeared, hopping deftly across their path and making a noise like it was clicking its teeth. At once, the pig went wildly after it, chasing it this way and that, until at last the hare led the thing under the bridge, where it planted itself firmly, refusing to come out.

Tom pulled and shoved, but could not get the pig to budge from its place in the muck and water under the bridge. His clothes were soaked, and he was chilled to the bone, tired and hungry and spent, and somehow, the pig's strength was like the strength of twelve men. It was then that Old Betty came by again, strolling above the scene on the bridge. She leaned over to stare into Tom's mud-covered face and smiled down at him.

"Oh, poor cousin. What a hard run you've had. Let me take that troublesome animal off of your hands, won't you? Of course, it's so lean and ill-tempered. I suppose I could now pay a quarter of my original offer for it."

Tom was angry, but humbled and desperate, and he agreed to the deal, accepting a meager sum just to be rid of the whole thing. And they say that as Old Betty slid her rope around the sow's neck, it came willingly, as gentle an animal as ever there was, and she fattened it and bred it, and had a great many pigs from that sow over the years that followed.

Turning the Key
Scotland

A very long time ago, in the town of Skerray, there lived a midwife—sometimes called a *howdie* in those days—who had lent her fishing net to a neighbor that he might set out with it one day and return to share with her a portion of his catch in exchange. In the course of the day, however, the net went missing. All of the fishermen had stepped away, for they were spear-fishing for salmon, and when they returned, the net had vanished entirely. The midwife was vexed at this news, for the net was very fine and many yards long, and she had no intention of letting the matter be. "I'll find the thief," she said to her neighbor, "one way or the other."

And so she sent for a cunning man who was traveling about the area, for this man was quite famous as a sorcerer capable of locating stolen objects, and she knew that with his aid, the thief would be brought to justice. He came from Leitholm, which was quite a ways south, but he traveled about in those days, wandering from town to town, for his services were much desired.

When the cunning man arrived at the home of the midwife, he assured her that he could indeed locate the thief by means of a charm that he called *turning the key*. That evening, by candlelight, he and the woman gathered at her kitchen table, where he produced a bible, a length of thread, and a small key. He read aloud two passages from the bible, one of these being the tale of Saul and the Witch of Endor. He tied one end of the thread to the key itself, then tucked the thread and key into the bible so that the handle end of the key was sticking out. The key was then to be held between the midwife's fingers as she recited the names of the suspected thieves out loud.

Having read a long list of names, all being fishermen present when her net was stolen, the cunning man was surprised to find that none of them were guilty. For the charm would give a loud and clear indication when the guilty party was named. At last, the midwife said, "Well, I'd never think it of him, but I've yet to name old Jock Wilson." And as soon as she pronounced his name, the bible and key came apart, the book landing with a loud thud and the key clinking against the floor, for the true thief had been named.

A Drink of Ash
Isle of Man

On the Isle of Man, the traditions of everyday charming and practical witcheries were not viewed quite as harshly as in Scotland and England. While these practices were still viewed as the work of the Devil, those found guilty were often jailed for a month or less, or sentenced to penance, and then released, more for annoying the authorities than for anything else.

Alice Knakill, in 1712, was found guilty of using certain charms that upset her neighbors. She was said to have taken a bit of earth from near her neighbor's doorstep, after which she burned it over a fire until it was reduced to ash, then fed it to one of her cows, with the goal of increasing its milk production—perhaps at the expense of her neighbor's prosperity. Another neighbor accused her of cutting or ripping away a piece of her petticoat, which she likewise burned to ash, then mixed into a beverage to drink herself. She said the purpose of the second charm was to restore health, and again, we must wonder whether this charm's operative magic was based on transference, of taking from one in order to give to the other. Ultimately, she was sentenced to penance over three Sundays.

In 1713, in the village of Ballaugh, a charm-woman by the name of Alice Cowley was found guilty of several counts of witchery. She was believed to have sold a charm to a young man for the purpose of causing women to fall in love with him. The charm was composed of a folded piece of paper, containing a strange powder made from certain stones. She was also believed to have helped women with problems of fertility, to ensure good harvests for farmers, and to increase the size of herds. She was sought after by those with sick children, and even by young women eager to find husbands. Ultimately, she was sentenced to thirty days' imprisonment, followed by a public display of penance.

In 1716, in the parish of Jurby, a vicar was called to rule in a matter of suspected witchery. It was brought before him that a husband and wife were seen walking early on the first of May, wetting their feet with the dew of that morning, which has long been believed to be a special day for witches and for old folk magic of many sorts. The couple were believed to have been working a charm on the crop to ensure its good harvest. The vicar, however, was merely annoyed, and announced a fine and forty days' imprisonment on anyone who brought such matters before him again.

Turn and Spin
New World

A great long while ago, in the vast swamplands of Louisiana, poor folk lived hard lives, surviving by the skin of their teeth. And it so happened that there lived a man who earned his wages transporting goods here and there on long journeys through the swamps on his little boat, often overnight, earning only enough to keep himself from the jaws of hunger.

One night, on one of his more arduous journeys, the man was so very tired and had eaten so little that he found himself quite weak and faint, and he felt he could go no further without a rest. And so he slept for a bit on his little boat, with only the lantern beside him to keep its dim vigil, for the old trees of the swamp blotted out even the light of the moon and stars, such that it was utterly dark all around him.

When he awoke, he had no way of knowing where he was and how far his little boat had drifted in the swamp's endless darkness, and the candle in his lantern was all but spent, and he knew that he would be lost and much afraid should he not find a place to stop before the candle had gone out. What's more, a terrible hunger was upon him, for he had not eaten in several days, and his stomach groaned and pained him greatly.

It was then that he caught whiff of an old, familiar smell, that of bacon frying and hot cornbread fresh from the oven, which shook him from his weariness and also quickened his pace, for nearby, he knew, must be an old stilt house somewhere in the swamp, and someone cooking inside, and they may be kind enough to allow him some food and rest in exchange for work.

Following his nose, the poor man came at last upon the house, which was humble in appearance but very well-kept, and he docked his little boat and watched to see who walked by the window. For if the home belonged to a Black family, it was surely safe to knock upon the door, but if it belonged to white people, he would not. Thankfully, he saw a creole woman walk by the window, and so he knew it was likely safe, and she beckoned him to come inside, remarking that he looked so very weary and hungry. And he was speechless before her, for she was quite beautiful, and she offered him bacon and cornbread and anything else he wanted, and once he had fed and calmed himself, the two of them talked long into the night, until at last, the poor man, thoroughly sated, fell asleep on her floor.

The next morning, the kind woman prepared for him yet another fine meal of fried eggs and buttery grits and fresh biscuits, which was once again some of the best food the poor man had ever tasted in his life. She invited the man to stay for a time, for she was happy to have the help around the house. He obliged, of course, and the longer he stayed with her, the healthier and happier he became, until at last the woman told him that she was in love with him and wished him to stay forever. He was only too happy to agree to this, and though it would be nice to say it was for love, the truth is seldom so kind as what we wish, and the man stayed in greater part for his own comfort.

As days and nights passed, however, the man noticed something strange. Anytime he woke in the middle of the night and looked beside him in bed, the woman was gone, and was nowhere to be found in the house. When he rose in the morning, she would be beside him once more. This went on for quite some time, until at last, the man decided he simply must know where his generous patroness went in the dark of the night.

And so the following evening, as they retired to bed as usual, the man pretended to sleep, snoring and lying as still as he could, until at last he felt her get up from her side of the bed, and squinting one eye, he watched her make her way to the fireplace in the other room. There, she replenished the fire with fresh wood and pushed her old spinning wheel near its warmth, and she sat herself down and began to spin.

It was not wool she spun, though; she simply turned the wheel, closing her eyes and moving strangely, humming to herself, until at last she began chanting the strange words:

Turn and spin. Come off, skin.
Turn and spin. Come off, skin.

And with those words, the flesh of her hands began to loosen and wind itself about the wheel, which pulled the skin from her arms away, and then the skin from her body, and then the skin of her head and face and legs and all, until finally, all of her human skin was wound about the wheel, and her hidden form underneath it was revealed: that of an enormous tabby cat. She gathered the skin up carefully, folded it neatly, and placed it under the bed where the man was sleeping. And with that, she leapt through the window, flying through the cool evening air until she landed on a tree, and so went off into the night, flying from tree to tree, as no earthly cat could do.

The man sat up in bed then, his eyes wide with shock at the sight he had just seen, for he knew now that this was no ordinary woman, but a witch woman. Now, the man had heard from the old people many tales of witching folk: how they make deals with the Devil, how they will take a man's virility, or steal babies, or other awful things, and though we would, of course, like to believe that the man acted only to preserve his life from danger, what must have played in the back of his mind was also the comfort of the little house and his new life, and of how, if he were rid of the witch, he could have it all to himself and take a new wife who was not of the witching sort.

So he took out the witch's skin from under the bed, unfolded the thing, and turned it inside out. He took salt from the cabinet and sprinkled it all over, rubbing it into every crevice of the witch's human skin, then folded it once more and placed it under the bed again, just as it was. Then he lay back in bed for a long time, his eyes closed, pretending to snore again, waiting for the cat to return.

When it finally did, it landed silently on the windowsill, then carefully crept across the floor, kissing the man gently on the forehead before retrieving the skin from under the bed. It would be nice to say that the man felt a pang of guilt, then, for witch women can love, of course, just as strongly as other women, but in truth, his mind raced already with the thoughts of selling her things, of what price he might get for this or that, and of how he might buy new clothes and present himself to young women so that he might take a new love to a house that he himself now owned.

The great tabby cat attempted to climb back inside the skin, but the salt annoyed and itched terribly, and it could not stand it for long, and so the poor thing climbed in and out, and in and out again, and the man, lying in bed, could not help himself but to laugh, at which the tabby cat looked at him, its eyes wide with shock. It jumped through the window, disappearing once more into the trees, and was gone.

And so, the man was left with the home and property and all the comforts thereof all to himself, and the witch never returned after that. But considering the man had become dependent on her kindness for nearly everything in his life, and was not quite the catch he imagined himself to be, it is unlikely that he married again, nor that he made much of his treasures.

The Witch's Creel
Scotland

It was on the Isle of Lewis, which lies on the western side of Scotland, that some of the most powerful wind-witches were known in ages past. Their abilities to call on the winds were legendary, such that they could sell a portion of wind, often sealed in magic knots, to passing merchant ships. Those who won their favor always had a safe voyage, while those they held in contempt were swallowed by the salt sea in sudden storms, which came without sign or warning.

In those days of the old, legendary witches of Lewis, there lived on the island a tailor who traveled about for his business, mending clothes and fitting garments for those who could afford his services. He was summoned to the home of a local, well-to-do farmer who had prospered for many years, and after his work was completed, the tailor was politely invited to stay for the night, for it had grown quite late in the evening.

Much to his surprise, the dinner served that night was a simple one, with bread and vegetables plenty, but no fish. This was an odd thing, for fresh-caught herring was a staple on the island, and was usually to be expected on the table when serving guests. Still, the tailor smiled and ate his meal politely, making no mention of the lack of herring.

After they had finished their meal, the farmer excused himself to go and retire to bed, but his wife lingered, sipping her ale and smiling at the tailor as if she held some secret. "You noticed, of course, that there was no herring," she said to him from her chair beside the fire.

"I did, indeed," replied the tailor.

"There has been poor fishing of late, and it has been difficult to find."

"A shame," he replied, "for a meal without herring is a sad affair."

The farmer's wife leaned forward in her seat. "If you will make me a promise this night, I'll make you one in return. Pretend to go to bed as usual, but say no prayers to God. Rise when the moon is high, and meet me here by the fire with some of your strongest worsted yarn, and we shall bring back the greatest haul of fish, and you shall take half of it with you when you leave this house tomorrow."

The tailor thought this matter strange, especially the bit about neglecting his evening prayers, but he promised nonetheless and did as the farmer's wife requested, pretending to go to bed that night, only to rise when the moon was in the sky. He crept down the stairs slowly by the light of his candle, stopping once he realized it was not only the farmer's wife waiting for him below, but a great number of women, all standing silently, waiting for his arrival. Each held an empty fishing basket in their hands.

"Well-spotted, sister," said one of the women to the farmer's wife, who was standing among them. "This one will do nicely for the charm tonight."

It was then that the tailor realized that he stood before the powerful witches of Lewis, and that the farmer's wife was one among their very number. He felt a shiver of fear then, for while the Lewis witches were not known to be needlessly cruel, they were capricious, their moods shifting as quickly as the island's weather, turning from kindly to murderous in an instant if even a hint of an insult was given or perceived.

"How then can I aid you good women this night?" said the tailor nervously, minding his manners. "We are to go fishing, I presume?"

The whole lot of the witches broke into laughter then, their cackles bubbling and churning like the crests of waves.

"Fishing indeed," replied the farmer's wife, "though not as you might suppose. Have you brought me your strongest worsted yarn?"

"As promised," he said, and handed her the yarn.

"And have you said no prayers this night to God, not to the Father, the Son, or the Holy Ghost?"

"I've said no prayers," he said, though he suddenly wished that he had.

The sea-witch smiled, evidently pleased, and passed the yarn to another in her company. She then leaned down to the fireplace and blew therein, and a great crackling fire started up that instant, though its light was pale and strange, like no fire lit by man.

"The yarn of a tailor without prayer on his lips," said one witch, drawing a length of the fiber.

"The creel of a fisherman, empty of fish," said another witch, setting an empty fishing basket before the fireplace.

It was then that the farmer's wife picked up the basket and tied a knot on its handle, then drew a length of the yarn, then tied another basket on, and so on and so forth until nine baskets were tied with the yarn on their handles, all along one length of the tailor's worsted yarn.

"Hold this end of the yarn," said the farmer's wife to the tailor, passing him the very end of it, "and do not let go no matter what you see or hear."

And by the light of that witch-fire, as pale and iridescent as abalone, the room appeared strange, and all sense of up and down seemed to dissolve and swirl, and in the eddy of his vision, there seemed to be no room at all anymore, only an endless expanse of watery abyss before him, with the moon hanging above, and he felt cold and dizzy then, and he held himself, shivering, floating in the bright space between worlds that the witches had rent.

And he saw the witches rising then, all in a row, not like birds in flight but like weightless, drifting figures, smiling and laughing as they went, their hair unfurling in the air around them as if they were underwater, though they were not, for they drifted up towards the moon and clouds, each with a basket in their hands that had been tied together with his own worsted thread.

One after another, the witches reached a pinnacle above him, and appeared to gesture and call at the very stars shining above, and when they did so, a stream of silvery fish would pour from the stars into a basket, filling it to the brim with fish. After every last basket was filled, the witches gently careened downwards, spiraling back, returning to where the tailor was, holding his end of the yarn, suspended on the edge of the rapturous expanse they had conjured.

But he felt a great and sudden terror then, as he saw the witches coming back towards him. What would become of him, now that he knew their secret and they had gotten the haul of fish that they wanted? Would they allow him to live? Even if they deemed it so, would he then be forced to serve them for the rest of his days?

And so the tailor took the scissors from his pocket, and he cut the yarn, and all of the witches fell screaming into the sea, cursing him as they did, and all of the fish fell with them, and the moon became dark, and darkness encroached all around him, until at last he found himself standing before the unlit fireplace in the farmer's house, alone.

Needless to say, the tailor left that house that very night to return to his own home, caring not to stay a moment longer. He had poor luck fishing for the rest of his days, never catching a single fish on his own, and often being met with terrible storms at sea. This went on for such a long time that the tailor eventually refused to step on any boat at all, and lived the rest of his life with his two feet planted at all times on solid land, lest the wrath of the Lewis witches find him at last.

The Witch's Braid
Ireland

Many ages ago, in the time of castles, kings, giants, and witches of all sorts, some kind and others fearsome, there lived a young prince who wished to embark from his father's castle and journey across the land on his own, to make of his own fate what he would, come what may. Though his mother pleaded and his father threatened, nothing could persuade the young prince from his heart's desire for adventure.

And so he left his father's great castle, leaving behind the safety of the king's men and those great walls, and all the fineries and comforts of his life before, and he made his way across the land on horseback to seek his own fortune. The road grew rough and narrow, and before long, he found himself in a dark, dark wood, so thick that he could not see the sky above, and indeed had no way of knowing if it was day or night, or in which direction he was traveling.

At last, he came to a little cottage tucked away in the forest. Its old thatch roof was in disrepair, but the smoke billowing from its crumbling chimney told him that someone must be home to answer the door, and he was badly in need of rest and warmth. But strange things live in the dark forests of the world, and appearances are often deceiving, or so his mother had told him. Nonetheless, he was exhausted and shivering and without a clear path out of the wood, and so he knocked upon the door.

It was an old woman with long, silvery hair who answered, and she bid him come inside and sit by the fire. She offered him food and drink, and as they sat together and talked, they became fast friends, and she told him that her little cottage was not far at all from the other edge of the wood, and that he was within two hours' ride of a great neighboring kingdom. "A savage place," she called it, "with no respect for oaths."

"Why do you say that?" asked the young prince.

"Tomorrow be the first of many bloody days," explained the old woman. "The king's daughter has been promised to a giant, but the king himself has decreed that any young man who can kill the giant shall have his daughter's hand. Many will die needlessly. Such fools men are."

"Fools indeed," said the young prince with a chuckle, though he secretly decided that very moment that he himself would fight the giant and have the maiden's hand for himself.

"Take your rest here," offered the old woman, "and leave once the fighting is done, for the roads will be swarming with bandits in the meantime. I will be away during the day to gather herbs in the wood, and you will have the cottage to yourself for some much-needed rest."

The young prince agreed and thanked her for her offer, and the next day, as soon as the old woman left with her satchel to gather her herbs, he traveled on through the wood to the neighboring kingdom. There gathered all manner of knights and princes and young lords, all waiting for the chance to fight the giant for the hand of the king's daughter, who was indeed a great beauty and the daughter of a wealthy and proud family. But it was the prince at last who was chosen to fight the giant, for he was beautiful himself, and the princess was taken with him above all others.

And such was the prince's skill in battle that he slew the giant with little effort, leaving the great heap of him in a bloody pile upon the ground. Having been victorious in battle, he expected to embrace the king's daughter with a kiss, but the king raised his hand to halt him in his tracks, and he explained to the young prince that two other giants would come to claim the princess, and he must defeat these other two as well. Only then would the couple be free to marry.

The young prince thought this no challenge at all. He had so easily dispatched the first giant, what of two more? And so he returned to the old woman's cottage in the wood to take his rest for the evening, and planned to return the next day to repeat the ordeal.

When he entered the front door, however, he found the old woman holding her face and weeping pitifully beside her fire. "My son!" she cried mournfully, "My darling boy! How could they mutilate you so! I thought my spell would hold fast for you, to preserve your life against these savages! How could this have come to pass?"

The young prince quickly realized the precarious situation at hand, for his host was none other than the witch-mother of the giant he had slain that very day. He pretended not to hear the old woman's cries, and slammed the door loudly to make it sound as if he had only just entered the little cottage.

"Oh," upstarted the old woman, drying her tears quickly, "How goes your day, my boy? I've stew on the fire. Please help yourself first. You are my guest."

"What has happened, good woman?" asked the young prince, slyly. "Have you been weeping?"

"It is nothing to bother you with, sweet boy," replied the old woman. "You've no remedy for my sorrow. We shall talk of other things."

And so this cycle of events became a pattern over the next two days: the prince would set off in the morning, after the old witch went out to pick her herbs, and he would slay another of her sons, and then return in the evening, avoiding all suspicion, until at last, he had slain the last of the giants, and the king told him to return home for the last time, and that on the next day, there would be a great feast to celebrate his victory and a wedding to follow immediately after. But as fate would have it, the young prince left in such a gleeful hurry that one of his shoes fell off onto the street, and he arrived at the old woman's cottage with only one shoe.

"My, you've lost your shoe, dear boy," remarked the old woman through her tears as they sat down to supper. Her eyes were red from weeping, and her face was pale and drawn with grief. "How did you lose it when you were only roaming around the cottage while I was gone?"

"I've not a clue," said the young prince, slyly. "I'm sure it's around here somewhere."

"We'll find it together, I'm sure," said the old woman, who was surely exhausted from mourning the deaths of all three of her sons. "I've gathered enough herbs to last the winter now, so I'll be home all day tomorrow. We'll find your shoe, and then you can be on your way safely, so that you might leave me to my grief."

For several days, the old woman searched around the property for the shoe, and the prince of course pretended to search for it, knowing full well that it must have fallen onto the street after slaying the witch's third son in battle. All the while, the king's men were conducting their own search for the owner of the shoe, for he had promised to marry the king's daughter, but had quite disappeared without a trace.

At last, the king's men came to knock upon the cottage door, and they presented the young man's lost shoe and congratulated him on slaying all three of the witch's sons. Upon realizing that her guest, whom she had cooked and cleaned and cared for an entire week, was in fact the murderer of all three of her sons, the witch began to wail loudly, and as she wailed, her eyes turned yellow and cruel, and her fingers lengthened into claws, and her spine stretched, until she was towering over the prince.

"My curse be upon you, boy," cried the witch, her yellow eyes full of tears. "Darkness take you, and darkness bind you. May all hope fly from your grasp. And in your moment of terror, may none be there to aid you or to mourn you after." And with that, the witch transformed herself into a wild hare and leapt away into the wood.

But princes being princes, the young man soon forgot the witch's curse and lost himself completely in the pleasures of his new life as a husband and an heir to a wealthy kingdom. The newlywed couple took a smaller castle near the edge of the wood, and there they began building a life together, sharing happy days and all the comforts and luxuries they could want.

It was not long, however, before the servants began reporting the presence of a strange hare on the castle grounds. It would make its way through windows or pipes into the castle walls, and wherever it was seen, some disaster would soon follow: a fire would break out, or a tower would collapse, or someone would slip on the stairs and break their neck. What's more, the hare was said to have large yellow eyes, strange and twisted as if by rage.

The prince knew, then, of course, that the witch-hare would not stop hunting him until it spelled his very doom, and rather than risk his young bride, who was now with child, he set off to hunt the thing in the dark, dark wood. And princes being princes, he felt utterly sure of his imminent victory. He had slain three giants, after all. What challenge could a witch-hare possibly be for such a fierce warrior as he? The poor fool set off then, to kill at last the grieving mother of the three sons he had murdered previously.

Though he tracked the witch-hare all day and night through the dark wood, he could not land a single arrow upon it, and as he followed it through the twisted trees, it was evident that he was being led deeper and deeper into the impenetrable darkness of the forest, away and away until he had lost sight of his horse, until at last he was cold and weary and utterly spent, and he found himself at the old, dilapidated cottage where he had first met and deceived the witch. He had little choice but to set up there for the coming night, and for the first time, the young prince felt the prick of fear, and felt perhaps less than sure of himself, and he almost, though not quite, regretted killing the witch's sons in the first place.

The night was black as pitch in the depths of the forest, and the air was silent. Gone were the sweet sounds of frogs and crickets singing, of nightbirds sounding their calls. There was only a slight breeze, cold and wet, which sounded, against the stones of the old cottage, much like a mournful wailing in the utter darkness of the woods.

Sometime after midnight, the prince was awoken by a soft knock upon the door. It was a little old woman—not the witch he was expecting, but a pitiful, shivering thing. "Won't you please let me in, sir? I'm so very cold and tired from my journey. I only wish for a place to rest for the night, then I will be on my way."

"Good woman, I would," said the prince, nervously, "but there be a powerful witch in these woods. How am I to know that you will not harm me, if I should let you in?"

"A stranger's welcome is a sacred thing, is it not?" replied the old woman. "A curse on any guest who would betray a gracious host."

"Right you are, good woman," said the fool prince, and opened the door to let her inside.

"But first," said the old woman, "so that I know that *you* will not harm *me,* please take this braided cord of mine, and tie it about bow, your knife, and your sword, and then I will know you are a gentleman, and I'll have no fear."

And so the prince tied the braided cord around all three of his weapons, and as soon as he did so, the old woman stepped inside, and as she emerged through the doorway of the little cottage, she grew in size. Her hands stretched into long fingers with black, pointed nails, and her head loomed high above him, her silvery hair coiling down the length of the cottage, from floor to ceiling. As the prince gazed into her yellow eyes, he knew that he had fallen into the witch's snares after all.

"Come, bow!" he cried, reaching for his weapon.

"Bound be thine bow," the witch's voice cracked like thunder, and the bow, tied with her magic braid, flew out the window into the darkness of the wood.

"Come, sword!" he cried, reaching for his second weapon.

"Bound be thine sword," the witch's voice broke over the cottage like a great flood, and the sword, tied with her magic braid, flew out the window into the darkness of the wood.

"Come, knife!" he cried, reaching for his last weapon.

"Bound be thine knife," the witch's voice rang out, as cold and stony as the grave, and the knife, tied with her magic braid, flew out the window into the darkness of the wood.

"Please, please, spare my life!" he cried at last. "I am prince of this land and shall one day be its anointed king!"

The witch gazed over the sniveling, small sum of the prince with her yellow eyes. "Once, perhaps," she said at last. "Just as I was once a mother. Until I took a stranger into my home, and warmed his bones, and fed his hunger. But we are both changed now, you see. We will never again be what we were."

And as the witch fell upon him in her bloody rage, the scream that escaped from the prince's throat echoed through the wood, off its old trees and stones and hills. So shrill was his cry that the birds stirred in their nests, and young fawns perked their ears, and the princess, far away in her castle, hands cradled about her pregnant belly, felt a chill breeze enter her chamber from the open window, a draft of night air that almost sounded like a wail.

'Tis cold tonight, she thought to herself, and drew up her shawl around her.

Witch-Tracks
New World

In the old days, the suspicion against witches ran high, and even good charmers and healers, and even some folks with no knowledge of witchery at all, could be accused of practicing the hidden art. Most interesting of all is the assortment of sorceries known to detect and deter witches, all of these implements being of the same manner of craft said to be practiced by witches themselves—an irony sometimes lost on the practitioners of such counter-magics.

Such was the case many generations ago on a small family farm in New Hampshire, when the woman of the house was hosting a guest for the afternoon. They sat outside, enjoying cold drinks and discussing this and that, when a strange woman approached them from the road, asking for directions to the nearest town. The host gave the odd stranger the directions she requested, and the woman left on her way.

Whether it was from the traveler's disheveled clothing, her odd manners, or the fact that there was but one road between the one town and the other, we cannot say, but the woman of the house immediately suspected the stranger of being a witch, and she decided right then and there to determine whether it was true.

She took a long needle from her knitting basket, and followed the stranger back out toward the road a bit until she found a clear footprint left by the woman's shoe in the dirt. There, she planted her needle, sliding it straight through the footprint and into the ground. By this act, she said, any witch would be pinned to the spot, and could not move until the needle was removed again.

No sooner was the needle planted than the stranger, who had only just reached the road, stopped in her tracks. She stood perfectly still, then turned her head and stared at the woman and the needle stuck in the footprint. "Aha," said the woman, thinking that she had caught herself a witch after all, but at that very moment, the stranger lifted her foot and continued on, then disappeared down the road.

"I broke the spell, you see," said the woman of the house to her guest. "For one must be careful of speaking when working such charms; if the wrong word be uttered, or sometimes any word at all, the charm is undone, and it will not hold. That woman is a witch for sure, but there's nothing for it now."

Winter's Imps
England

It was commonly believed that the old witching folk entered agreements with familiar spirits, entities that sometimes took the form of animals, but would just as frequently take the form of imps, devils, and spirits of unearthly shapes, resembling no animal found in nature.

Once, a great many generations ago, in the village of Aldborough, there lived a witch-man, or wizard, who was notorious among the townsfolk for his knowledge of the dark arts. He went by the name of Winter, and he was said to keep a great many familiar spirits, tasked with bringing him secret knowledge, or tormenting his enemies, or aiding him in solving any problem at all.

Now, the power of witchcraft is one thing, but the power of gossip is another. And so it happened that a local farmer, having had several years of poor harvest, began to loudly and publicly blame Old Winter for his poor luck. He claimed to have seen him casting a blight upon his crops, cursing the very soil, and he even claimed that the witch-man had cursed his ploughman so that he could only ever operate the plough when standing on his hands with his legs in the air, a claim that was perhaps difficult for people to believe.

It was not long before the townsfolk began laughing at the old farmer's claims of being bewitched. They thought him mad, or perhaps thought he was making a mockery of them all with his nonsensical stories. Some even suspected that the old man was claiming to be cursed for the sake of pity, so that others may be more willing to help him in his plight.

Boldly, the farmer announced to the village one day that he would go to visit Old Winter himself that very night, and that he would return with proof that he and his farm had been witched. And so, having drunk more than his share of whisky to steel his nerves, he journeyed that night to the old wizard's house, which was not the estate of a wealthy man, but a humble cottage. Smoke drifted from the chimney up into the black night sky, and the farmer wondered then if he had perhaps made a mistake by arriving so late unannounced, but he shook off this thought, for it was surely too late for second-guessing.

He knocked upon the cottage door, but there was no answer. *The old witch-man is ignoring me*, thought the farmer, who grew even more perturbed. Being quite drunk, it did not occur to him that perhaps the old man simply did not hear the knock, and he imagined the wizard laughing inside his house, just as the townsfolk had laughed at him, and the thought enraged him, boiling his blood, and in a moment of anger, he decided to open the door and let himself in, come what may.

What he saw there inside the old wizard's cottage froze him dead in his footsteps, unable to move out of terror. There was the old witch-man, sitting at his table by the fireplace, whispering to a half-dozen creatures perched upon it, who seemed to twitter and click their mouths in response to him, conversing in some strange language. They were small and black, rodent-like, and somewhat reminiscent of bats, but in truth, they resembled no animal known to man.

When Old Winter saw the farmer standing in the doorframe, he spoke a strange word to the imps, who did not disappear, but appeared to float down through the table's surface, through the floor, presumably all the way down through the crust of the earth from whence they came. The look on Old Winter's face, his woolly brow furrowed in rage, sent the old farmer into a great fear then, and he ran straight home, not looking behind him.

Many of the townsfolk attempted to visit the old farmer after that night, curious as to what had happened during his visit with Old Winter, but none were allowed inside. The farmer would open the door, but all along its threshold on the floor, the old man had scattered ashes, and had drawn strange signs, circles and triangles and words that he claimed would keep all witching folk from entering, so long as they remained undisturbed. The old farmer became a recluse from then on, never leaving his home except when necessary, and even then, he could be heard muttering charms to protect himself from invisible dangers.

Some say that the old witch-man had cursed the farmer after all, but that he had cursed him with madness for spreading such nasty rumors about him. Others claimed that the farmer had been right from the start, and that the wizard had indeed ruined his farm, and continued tormenting him long after, which would drive anyone mad. Still others say that the farmer was an old drunk who spelled his own misfortune, imagining enemies where there were none, and driving himself to paranoia.

Perhaps the truth died with the farmer and that old wizard, in which case, we must decide on our own what to believe.

The Black Sheep
Scotland

Once, in another age, somewhere near the beach of Traigh Nan Gilean, there lived a young man who was set upon by strange forces at night. No sooner would he lay his head to his pillow than his rest would be interrupted by visiting spirits, and these events went on for so long that the man became truly miserable for lack of sleep.

Sometimes the spirit would visit him in the shape of a great black cat, which yowled and stared at him, and could not be sent away. Other times, the spirit took the form of a black crane, spreading its wings before him, which was frightening. Often, the spirit was simply a figure cloaked in darkness, which led the young man to believe that he was being visited not by a rotation of spirits, but by a witch, for witches often take as many forms as they choose.

Having given up the quest for sleep in his own bed, the man took to wandering up and down the beach of Traigh Nan Gilean, watching the moonlight and starlight shimmer on the water, and it was on one of these long nightly walks that he saw something strange. A sheep with a coat as black as night stood on the water's surface, as surely as if the water were stone under its hooves, and began walking towards him. Its pace became faster and faster, until at last the black sheep was sprinting towards him, and he knew this must be the witch, who had at last found him along the beach when she could not find him in his own bed.

And so the young man took a silver sixpence from his pocket, and he loaded it into his gun like a bullet, for it is known that an ordinary bullet cannot harm a witch. He fired the thing at the black sheep then, and he hit his mark, for the animal fell over just as it reached the shore, and where it fell, there lay a young woman draped in black fabric, holding the bullet wound in her leg.

He rushed towards her then, and he felt perhaps a mixture of things, for the woman was quite beautiful, and as she wept salt tears into the salt sea, he felt sorry that he had hurt her so. She beckoned him closer, and she told him that he must keep her secret, for if the people of the area knew she was a witch, she would be persecuted and killed for sure. And looking into her pleading eyes, he questioned then whether the witch had been visiting him out of malice at all, for no matter what frightening form she took on all the nights before, she had never hurt him as he had done her with his silver sixpence bullet.

In the weeks that followed, the young man did indeed keep the witch's secret, and he was able to sleep again at night, and all seemed well. This went on for a while, until one night, when the young man had more than his fill of whisky, he accidentally spilled the secret of the witch and the story of their meeting, and all present at the pub that night were shocked, and became maddened with rage, and demanded that the witch be found and killed.

It is unclear how the witch came to know that the young man had broken his promise, but find out she did, for witches have their ways of sniffing out such things. And the day came when the young man was off at sea on a bit of fishing, and there came a storm quite unexpectedly, a darksome line of clouds which surrounded the boat, and the young man and all aboard the vessel were drowned.

A Binding Horn
Wales

One of the famous Welsh sorcerers of old went by the name of Huw Llwyd, and his powers were renowned far and wide. He was said to have knowledge of every grimoire and magical book known to man. He was the seventh son of a seventh son, which amplified his abilities and inclined him towards greatness in the witching ways. And he had, himself, conducted one of the lesser-known rituals of old, eating the flesh of an eagle, which gave him and his descendants healing powers over the shingles and many other ailments besides. It is said that he used the following charm in his healing craft:

> *Male eagle, female eagle,*
> *I send you over nine seas,*
> *Over nine mountains,*
> *Over nine acres of wasteland,*
> *Where no hounds shall bark,*
> *Where no cow shall low,*
> *Where no eagle shall rise.*

So well-known were his abilities that one would think that Huw Llwyd would be met with welcome and good manners anywhere he went, but this was not always the case. It happened once, at an inn located in the village of Pentrefoelas, that Huw Llwyd was approached by four men who wished to join him for supper. They sat at his table without asking his permission, and acted as if they were all fast friends, and sought to make conversation about this and that with the sorcerer. Unfortunately for them, however, the conjuror was no fool, and he knew by the hidden sight that these men meant to kill him and rob him during the course of the night once he had fallen asleep.

After he finished his supper and his ale, just before Huw Llwyd retired for the evening, he cast a strange charm upon the would-be robbers. He conjured a horn, which grew out of the center of the table, from the very wood, and he compelled them to gaze upon it with all of their attention, and with all of their faculties to hold it in their sight. The men could do naught else, and they remained seated at that table all through the night, compelled by the strength of his craft. And so Huw Llwyd slept as soundly that night as ever, and in the morning, the men were still seated there, transfixed by the horn he had conjured to hold them.

The Witch-Deer
New World

It was many years ago, during a season of fine hunting in eastern North Carolina, that a group of men had gathered to discuss the subject of witchcraft. Over the course of several weeks, every hunter had spotted a certain strange deer in the swamps, which would stop and stare at them with its oddly shaped eyes, not moving a muscle. No dogs could catch it, no noise would scare it, and no bullet could injure it. And at last, it was agreed by all that this was no ordinary deer, but a witch-deer, for witches often take the form of nature's creatures in order to wander through the wilds in disguise.

From among their number, several hunters were selected, those believed to be the best shot with a rifle, and these men stationed themselves along the deer trails, but alas, even their bullets could not take down the witch-deer. In the end, it was decided that one hunter, the very best shot among them, should wait along the path where the creature always seemed to stop to rest, and he should fire at it with no ordinary bullet, but one made of silver, which they had purchased together and melted down themselves.

Now, it was believed that the true identity of the witch was a local, elderly woman who lived in a log house on the edge of the swamp, just a short walk from the closest road. Though the house stood in disrepair, those few who paid a visit to the woman found her ways strange, her home full of odd remedies, bones, and charms. One wonders what real harm this witch could possibly have done them, even if she did occasionally interrupt their hunting with her long walks through the swamp. But I digress.

The hunter took to his appointed task early one morning, waiting in the swamp where the witch-deer had been seen previously, and when it appeared and his shot was clear, he fired the silver bullet, which hit the creature as squarely and surely as anything. It ran off that day, and was never seen in the swamps again. And oddly enough, they say that the old woman of the swamp was seen with a limp in the weeks that followed, as if she had injured her leg, though she did not die of her ailment, living for a long time after.

One wonders, though, about the fate of those hunters in the years that followed, for every witch of those old times, at least in that part of the country, knew how to curse a rifle so that it could never again hit its mark, or even how to undo a man's luck for the rest of his life, or many other worse things besides. Such things did happen.

Whitethorn and Crossroads
Cornwall

It happened once in the village of Sancreed, and this was some time ago—though not as long as one might think—that a farmer had a number of dairy cows to sell, and so was taking offers in order to make a tidy profit. His neighbor, a woman reputed to be a witch by the locals, came forward with her own offer for the lot of them, and although the offer was fair and generous, the farmer refused, most likely because of her reputation, and he ultimately decided to sell to another farmer in the area, a man by the name of Jemmy, who was well-liked and did not suffer the same ill reputation.

Upon hearing of this, the woman began cursing Jemmy's name loudly and publicly, boasting that she would "pray to the powers" that his purchase should prove regrettable. Nor was this mere talk, for by her own account, the witch claimed that she had gone to an old whitethorn tree by a crossroads, and had prayed to the spirits there at night for their aid in casting the spell that would curse the cows.

It was shortly after this that Jemmy, the farmer who had purchased the dairy cows, experienced some trouble. They had all come into their milk, but that milk was sour and spoiled, having only a thin skin of rancid cream at the top, and so their milk was utterly useless to him. The farmer who sold him the cows would not believe this at first, but when he went to milk the creatures himself, he found it to be true, and he was forced to take back the lot of them and return the man's money.

Upon hearing of this ill fortune, the witch made no denials or apologies, but was, in fact, quite proud of the fact that her curse had taken root, announcing to the village and to any who would listen that the man had gotten just what he deserved for refusing to sell to her in the first place out of his prejudice against her. Whether this helped or harmed her future dealings with the townsfolk is a matter of debate, of course.

A Witch's Promise
Scotland

On the Isle of Coll, a great many years ago, a man named Hector MacLean was traveling along a hilltop pass, and it was there he was assailed by strange powers. He had reached a rocky, treacherous portion of the path when a black sheep appeared. It ran at him, trying repeatedly to knock him from the rocky ledge, and so he yelled at the creature, and threatened it with his blade, and at last decided to run in order to escape it, making his way towards his home.

Unfortunately for MacLean, his path home from that place led him across an opening cut through the rock by a stream, which was treacherous and had to be crossed carefully, and it was here that the black sheep caught up with him and commenced its attacks, seeking to cause him to slip and fall. Realizing that he was close enough to call out for help, he whistled loudly, and his dog came running up the hill, chasing the black sheep away.

The thing would not yield so easily, however. The dog chased the black sheep around and around, snapping ferociously at its heels, until at last the creature lifted itself off the ground and into the air, and it became an old woman wrapped in black cloth, hovering above him in the night sky. "Show mercy, man, and call away your dog," said the witch, "and I shall make to you a promise. I will be your ally in right and in wrong, and I will be a friend to you from this moment on."

With some degree of difficulty, MacLean managed to restrain his dog, though the creature was disobedient and fought him the whole time. He told the witch that he could only hold the hound for so long, and he urged her to flee while she could, before his strength gave out. At last, the dog turned as if to snap at its own master, and the witch became a hare and dashed away, and though the dog tried to catch her, it could not, and she escaped.

Now, MacLean did not see the witch for many years, so many years that he had nearly forgotten about their encounter. During this time, he took on a new role as a servant man to a neighboring, well-to-do farm. And while all had been well on the farm for a very long time, it happened one day that the milking cows came into a strange state, producing little, if any milk, as if they were witched.

Having encountered one witch already, and thinking himself the one to get to the bottom of the problem, MacLean set out one night to watch the cows and see for himself whether they were being visited by a witch or not.

And just as the moon rose high up in the sky, there came the hare, the form of the witch from so many years before, and it hopped up to one particular cow and began to drink milk straight from its udder, which was a strange sight indeed.

"Did you not swear to be my friend, so many years ago?" MacLean asked the hare, at which it became the old woman instantly, milk running down her chin and a look of shock upon her face. He had only meant to remind her of her promise, but his dog heard him and came running, and upon seeing the witch, the thing set upon her once more, and she was forced to take flight as before to avoid its bite.

"To be your friend, yes, that was the promise I made," said the witch, floating weightlessly above him in the dark. "But how was I to know that you worked on this farm? Would you begrudge a poor witch a bit of milk?"

"Then be a friend now," replied MacLean, "and take your witchery to Arileod, for I'll not have the people here thinking that the witched cows are my fault."

"I cannot tonight," said the witch. "For someone in the house has said their prayers to God, and my powers of travel are limited. Tomorrow, I will do as you ask."

And the witch did indeed go on to Arileod the following night, and proceeded with her witchery on a farm there, stealing the milk from the cows, and opening the barn doors, and letting loose the calves, and making whatever variety of mischief brought her amusement. She kept her promise to Hector MacLean, in the end, and was a friend to him, in her own way. But all of us are who we are, truth be told, and so even in friendship, the witch was perhaps entitled to a bit of fun and to stir up the occasional trouble, so long as it caused no real harm to anyone.

Nine Bits of Iron
Isle of Man

Long ago, near the quiet port-town of Peel, they say there lived a charmer of old, a wise woman and healer who was known for her ability to cure even the gravest of ailments. And she did so by means of a specific charm involving nine bits of iron.

It happened once in Peel that a young couple were very distressed, for their daughter had taken with a strange illness that none could explain, let alone cure. Her neck suffered from a swelling that greatly distressed her, and none of the usual treatments had any effect. It was then that they sent for the old woman, knowing her reputation as a powerful charmer.

The wise woman produced from her person nine objects, each a piece of metal. Some appeared to be bits of an old poker for one's hearth. Others looked to be old nails, bent and worn. But all were made of iron, and they were nine in number. Every piece was aged and distressed from use, as if she had employed them many times over the years.

With these nine bits of iron, she rubbed the girl's throat, one piece at a time, while uttering strange charms and incantations with the old Catholic flavor to them, though they were not, the parents could tell, strictly Christian in their composition. Once the girl's throat had been rubbed with all nine pieces, she then moved about the house, administering the charm to the doorways, the walls, and even some of the furniture, each time rubbing all nine pieces, one at a time, while reciting her charms.

And after the charm-woman's visit, the girl is said to have recovered swiftly, and the swelling never presented itself again, as strange as it may sound.

Churn and Loom
New World

It was in a small, rural town in New England, many years ago, that there lived a woman who was said to be under assault by witches. Why she had been singled out, none could say. Perhaps she had refused to aid some stranger in need, or perhaps she had withheld her generosity from a neighbor when she could have been kind, or perhaps there was no reason at all, for it is known that witches do as they please.

In any event, she set one day to churning butter, which she did regularly, but found that the butter simply would not come. For a whole day she churned it, until she was quite exhausted and spent, but still there was no butter, and so she set the cream back in her ice house and gave up. On the second day, she resumed churning once more, cursing the witches under her breath for making her back and arms so sore, and still, the butter would not come. On the third day, she left the cream in her ice house and turned to her weaving instead.

But her weaving was similarly plagued, as if the loom were cursed as well. Her shuttle would slip through her hands constantly, as if it were coated in grease, and fall to the floor. And her threads would change positions, seemingly without reason, so that her weft threads were twisted and wound beyond explanation. In her frustration, she cried out, "So be it! If it be witched, I'll cast it into the fire and burn it to ashes, then!" And no sooner had she spoken this threat than she heard a gasp in the room, as if someone were startled, though there were none present, and upon taking up her shuttle once more, found the threads had untangled themselves.

She then fetched her cream from the ice house, and set it in the churn before her in order to try out this approach once more. "If this cream will yield no butter, then I'll boil the lot of it down to char!" she announced loudly, then set a pot over her hearth as if to heat it. Again she heard the gasp from the invisible stranger, and as soon as she resumed churning, she could feel butter forming as it should.

And so, in the years that followed, though the woman still maintained for the rest of her days that she was a target of the witches, she made it her custom to threaten anything that gave the appearance of being bewitched, whether with burning or drowning, and so she could drive the curse from anything she owned.

A Gull-Witch
Scotland

In the age of the legendary sea-witches of the Isle of Mull, there once lived a sailor who made his living at times as a fisherman and at other times transporting goods from one port to another, but was ever engaged in travel by water, a dangerous affair even in the best of times.

It so happened that this sailor had offended one of the witches of the island, which was a serious matter, for the witches of Mull were notorious for holding a grudge and seeking vengeance, particularly in the form of sudden storms, wind, and even murder by drowning. But he was handsome in his way, and he had caught the eye of another witch who cared for him. And so the man was kept safe from the one witch by the other, their powers matched.

Once, during a day at sea, when the man saw a dreadful rolling wall of dark clouds approaching, he knew that the offended witch would at last have her vengeance, having finally crossed his path on the waves, without the other witch to protect him from her wrath. When he tried to catch a wind to carry him to a nearby port, the witch appeared as a gull hovering above the boat, and so long as the gull remained there, no wind could fill the vessel's sails, but he was quite trapped, unable to move out of the way of the coming storm.

Just then, when death seemed to the sailor all but sure, there appeared another bird out of the clouds: a cormorant. This was the form of the other witch when she took flight, the one who loved him and sought to protect him. She flapped her great wings, and the sails began to fill once more, and she settled in the water just behind, in the wake of his boat, and guided the vessel away from the fast-approaching storm.

And so the sailor and his boat went unharmed that day, and both made their way across the water to a nearby port, the gull-witch above him crying out in rage and the cormorant-witch behind, protecting him, and on that day, thankfully, the one who loved him was stronger than the other.

The Staining Curse
Ireland

Witchery has long been the domain of the poor, the oppressed, and the abused—a means of seeking justice when the law of the land brings none. The wealthy and powerful may be protected from hunger and from the cold, but neither money nor privilege can shield the one from the powers of witchcraft.

It happened once, long ago, that there lived a wealthy merchant couple in the South of Ireland. They were a miserly pair, refusing all charity as their own riches grew and grew, until at last they lived as elegant a life as lords and ladies, even as they watched their neighbors starve. No efforts could soften their hearts. Children would approach them begging for food, and the wife would only scream at them to get out of her way, swinging her walking stick at them like a cudgel.

Despite the couple's ill reputation, there came on one peculiar day an old woman to their front door. It was the wife who answered. The old woman smiled politely and asked if she might have some food. "Anything would do," said the woman, "for I am so terribly hungry. A piece of bread, or even a handful of meal would be a kindness."

"Who do you think I am," replied the merchant's wife, "to be entertaining beggars at my door? Begone with you, and do not return."

The beggar woman only smiled politely and left, and the merchant's wife was glad to be rid of her. But the next day, the old woman returned once more.

"Please," said the frail old woman, "may I have a sip of milk? For I know that it is milking day, and surely you must have enough to spare a little."

"Go away, woman," spat the farmer's wife. "I told you yesterday, and I tell you again: you'll have none of my bread, nor milk, nor anything else. Begone with you, and do not return."

The beggar woman only smiled politely and left once more, and the merchant's wife thought that surely this was the end of the matter. But the next day, the old woman returned yet a third time.

"I beg you kindly," said the old woman, ever so meekly and pleadingly, "let me only rest here on your doorstep for a moment. I know you won't share your bread or your milk, but if only I might sit down for a bit and rest my bones."

At this third visit, the merchant's wife grew furious. "You stupid hag," she shouted, "I care not for your misery. If you don't drag yourself from my door this very moment, I'll fetch my cane and beat you to death."

"I'll leave you to your fortune, then," said the old woman, smiling slyly. But before she left, she placed one hand gently on the frame of the door and spoke some strange words under her breath that the merchant's wife could not understand. And then she was gone.

The merchant's wife was relieved to find that the old woman did not visit the next day, which she considered a blessing. She carried on with her day, strolling through her garden and enjoying the many luxuries her rich life afforded. It was in the afternoon that she found herself parched and possessed of a fierce craving for a drink of cold milk, so she went to the kitchen to fetch some.

As she poured the fresh milk into a cup, she noticed something small and black fall in with it, but try as she might to poke and prod and fetch it from the glass of milk, she could not get hold of the thing. Her thirst for the milk was so intense then that she gave up and drank the entire glass down, then another, and then another, until she was thoroughly sated.

Almost immediately, the symptoms began. It started with a terrible pain in her stomach, which then spread throughout her body. Eventually, her skin began to change a dark purplish color, like a terrible bruise, and this spread over her whole body. Doctors could find no cause or treatment. It was then that her husband sent for a local priest who was familiar with matters to do with witching folk.

"A witch's curse, for sure," announced the priest. The woman thought of the old beggar who visited her earlier in the week, and for the first moment in her life, regretted her cruelty, wishing she had been even kind enough to allow the woman to rest on her doorstep for a moment.

The priest put the merchant's wife into a bathtub of scalding hot water, which burned her skin terribly, and into this, he poured a measure of holy water, which burned all the more. Slowly, though, the stains on her skin began to recede, first from her feet, then from her legs, then from her torso and head, and then from her arms, until she looked quite like herself.

Upon stepping out of the tub, however, the merchant's wife noticed that one of her hands was still stained with the witch's curse. "Father," she said, "we must do it again, for the affliction still lingers here in my hand."

"Nothing else can I do for you," said the priest. "With God's blessing, you've been healed of the rest, but that marked hand, that is the portion of the witch's curse that even God himself deems fair punishment, and it will remain with you so long as your soul is stained with wickedness."

The woman was greatly grieved by her hand for a time, but eventually, she learned to live with it, often wearing gloves to hide it from sight. More importantly, she was quite changed after that, and sought to spend her fortune helping others, giving alms to the poor and aid to any neighbor who needed it, and they even say that many years later, after her death, they removed her gloves and found that the mark was at last gone from her hand, for she had done so much good that even the witch had forgiven her.

Hoof to Rail
New World

It happened long ago in New England that there lived a farmer, and because his sows had produced more young pigs than he intended to keep for his own farm, he decided to sell the remaining number to local households who wished to fatten them over the season.

One by one, the farmer sold the little pigs to this neighbor and to that neighbor, all for a fair price, until the last of the things had been sold, a total of ten in number. As was his custom, he held all of the pigs for the new owners until they were able to return the following day to cart them off. And all would have gone well by this plan, had a witch not shown up that very afternoon.

"Alas, good woman," the farmer said, "all of my pigs have already been sold and promised away."

"Are they? And don't I see ten young pigs, just there?" said the witch.

"Yes," replied the farmer, "but they have been paid for, and will be carted off soon. I cannot sell you what has already been sold."

The witch squinted her eyes then with annoyance, for she believed him to be lying. Mind you, it was often true that folk refused to have dealings with those suspected of being witches, and though this was not the case at hand, the witch most likely had had difficulty before with others about the town, and so she refused to believe his excuse.

"If you do not sell me one of those pigs this day," said the witch, "you will be sorry for it tomorrow."

The farmer, of course, could not very well fulfill her request, and so he sent her away empty-handed, and the witch turned with a scowl on her face and left back down the road the way she came, muttering to herself along the way. And though the man did not like the ominous tone of the woman's words, he perhaps thought the matter settled.

This was not the case. The next morning, the farmer walked out to feed the creatures, and what he found was a strange sight indeed. Half of the pigs had hopped onto the rail of the fence and were walking along its length in a line, putting one little hoof in front of the other in an impossible feat of balance. One by one, the remaining pigs joined them, until they were all walking along the fence rail. They went around it once, and then, one by one, all ten of them hopped down as gracefully as you please, and trotted off in a single-file line towards the edge of a nearby wood, and disappeared, and were never found again.

A Witch's Ladder
England

In the late 1800s, in a small town nestled in the tranquil fields of Somerset, a strange object was discovered. It was a length of rope, either stuck through or braided together with a great many feathers—from both crows and geese—so that they pierced the length of it at regular intervals, resembling, when allowed to hang, a kind of "ladder." It was called, and is still called to this day, a *witch's ladder*.

Charms of the old craft involving a series of knots, feathers, or pins are well-known, of course, in many variations, but it is the manner in which this object was discovered that sets it apart. It was found hidden in a small cottage, made in the old way with cob walls and a thatch roof, a dwelling said to be hundreds of years old. Unfortunately, the structure was so dilapidated and had fallen into such disrepair that the owners had no choice but to demolish it. When they did so, they discovered a secret room: a space between the thatch roof and the upper floor of the house, and in this space, among other things, were tucked several brooms and the witch's ladder.

When locals were questioned about the objects, opinions appeared to differ, and two distinct explanations were put forward. Some claimed that these objects were placed to propitiate the spirits of witches in the area (much in the way that one might leave offerings for the faeries), that they might favor the owners and bless their farm rather than curse it. The brooms placed in the space, under this interpretation, were left for the witches' enjoyment, and the "ladder" was set there to enable them to "cross over" into the hidden room just under the roof.

The second explanation, which is quite different from the other, was that the witch's ladder was an old charm referred to once as the "rope and feathers." A variant of the infamous "witch's knots," which were tied while uttering spells for various purposes, the "rope and feathers" was enacted similarly, a charm of repetition, each feather woven into the rope while uttering spells aloud. This charm existed in yet another variant, according to local knowledge, for witches may also stick pins in a candlestick—called the "candle and pins"—muttering charms as each pin goes in. All these charms may serve as vehicles, according to the tales, of the witch's will, whether for good or ill.

Yarn and Thread
Scotland

Thomas Grieve, a skilly man offering magical healing services in the kingdom of Fife, was tried for witchcraft in 1623. He was said to be able to heal any ailment of the body by drawing it out of the patient and taking it within himself, then casting it out onto an animal. He was also known to heal cows and other livestock by wrapping them in a charmed length of cloth, which would remain tied about them all night long, until the rising of the sun, at which point he would burn the cloth, and the illness would be gone. He healed human patients, supposedly, by passing them through a wide hank of yarn, which would then be cut and burned to take the illness with it.

Similarly, the accused witch Andrew Man was believed to have healed a man by passing the patient nine times through a hank of yarn, then passing a cat through the hank nine times as well. The cat, though, was passed through the hank backwards so that it would take on the sickness of the patient, after which it was believed to have become sickly and died, while the man was restored to health.

Isobell Straquhan, too, one of the accused witches of Aberdeen, was believed to have used fibers in her craft, sewing a variety of colored threads into pieces of paper until they were quite thick and vibrant, then placing them about the property of Walter Ronaldson. The man was, of course, a notorious wife-beater, and the charm was intended to end his assaults against his spouse. Many local people believed that the charm had achieved the desired result, and that the man beat his wife no more after that. And for this, Isobell was executed.

Wool of Red, Wool of Blue
Wales

Long ago, there lived an elderly couple who kept a small but tidy property in the countryside. They were neither rich nor poor, subsisting on their farm and the fruits of their own labor. The wife supplemented their modest income by dying a portion of their wool, which could be sold for a higher price in town or traded in order to fill in the gaps in what their little farm could produce.

And so it happened once on a wool-dying day, when the woman was engrossed in the task of preparing the submersion to dye a great heap of freshly cleaned wool, that a stranger appeared at her door. Her visitor was a very old woman, much her senior. She walked with a cane, and her long, white hair was set in a neat braid down her back.

"Share with me some of your blue dye, would you?" asked the old woman, "for I've none left of my own."

Her host thought for a second, then answered, "If only I could, good woman. But I've barely enough for my own wool. I cannot part with any." This was, of course, only half true, for she could easily have sold a smaller portion of blue wool, then acquired more dye to complete the rest of it later.

The older woman looked her up and down, squinting, but at last turned to leave, empty-handed. Before she departed the doorstep, though, she looked back over her shoulder and made a strange gesture with her hand. The farmer's wife thought nothing of this at the time, for after all, the very old are entitled to their strange ways.

As she resumed the work of dying her wool, strange things happened. Each time she removed the wool from the vat and washed it clean, it was found to be dyed red instead of blue. She repeated her task several times with the same effect, until at last she threw up her hands, thinking that she had been sold the wrong color.

She decided to pay a visit to the neighbor from whom she acquired the dye, but after explaining the strange turn of events, her neighbor did not believe her. "There is no fault in what I sold you," she said. "Let us each take a portion of wool and use the dye side-by-side, and you shall see."

And so they each took a portion of freshly cleaned wool, and they each dyed it in their own submersion prepared from the same dye, and the neighbor woman rinsed hers to reveal a deep blue, and the farmer's wife rinsed hers to reveal a bright red, just as before. Such a thing could not be explained by either of them, and they scratched their heads in disbelief.

"Have you, by chance, been visited by anyone recently?" asked her neighbor at last, "and did they ask you for anything at all, no matter how small?"

"Why yes," replied the farmer's wife. "Only yesterday I was visited by an old woman who asked for a portion of my dye, but I refused."

"Ah," replied her neighbor, "then she has surely set a curse of some sort. Let us test it, then, to see if it is the wool that has been cursed."

This went on for some time, testing this sample of wool and then that, and testing this portion of dye and then that, until at last it became clear that it was not the dye or the wool that was cursed, but the woman's very own hands. No matter what materials she used, no portion of wool would ever come out the color she intended.

But in this, she counted herself lucky, in the end. For to refuse a witch is a grave matter indeed, and many are those who have been cursed terribly, even unto sickness and death. The farmer's wife continued her trade for many years, dying her wool, then selling it at market or trading it for goods. But of course, she could never predict what color she would have next, and so when folks asked her what color wool she might have for sale the following week, she would simply say, "We'll see."

A Dark Blessing
New World

Somewhere along the old forests and mountains of Ontario, long ago, there lived a husband and wife who got on quite well and built a comfortable life for themselves together. The husband, however, did not get along with all, for by some misspoken word or absent-minded gesture of rudeness, he had offended a local woman many believed to be a witch. And the witch held this spite against him for a long time, nursing her grudge over the years, until at last it became a burning hatred, and it became well-known that the old woman wished the man nothing but ill fortune.

Over time, as the old woman's hatred became more and more bitter, odd changes began to manifest in the man. His face, which had once been friendly, became twisted and cruel, and his words, which had once been kind, became venomous, until at last he was unrecognizable. He began imagining enemies everywhere, and finally, in his madness, he turned on his own wife and made several attempts on her life.

Thankfully, his young wife was a clever one, and she was able to outwit and escape him each time. She fled their home, and the woman found shelter wherever she could, but eventually, no matter where she settled, the man would find her and would try to murder her once more. And it was after this went on for some time that neighbors and friends finally intervened, and they determined that the husband must have been bewitched into his madness, for no other cause could be found.

They caught him, and bound him, and brought him to the old woman, demanding that she remove the curse she had placed on his mind, but the witch refused, for the old grudge was still like a fresh wound to her.

"Very well," said one of the people, who knew something of witching ways. "If you will not remove the curse, simply say the words *God bless you*, and we will leave you be."

And this the old woman did, but not quite, for her exact words were, "*My* God bless you."

Well, no sooner was he released than the man went on as before, attempting to kill his wife yet again, for he was still stark-raving mad with the witch's curse. At last, some of the folk began to realize what had happened and why the spell was not broken, for it was long believed that the god of certain malevolent witches was none other than the Devil himself.

When they repeated the operation once more—bringing the bound man to her again, demanding that she say the exact words *God bless you*—the old witch gave up her scruples, being tired of the whole affair, and said the words correctly, just as they asked. Perhaps, in the end, the witch hated so many uninvited guests knocking on her door more than she loved holding onto her grudge, but who can say? At any rate, they say that once she spoke the words, the darkness left the man's eyes at once, and he was as before the madness took hold, if such things be believed.

Hair and Nails
England

In England, even long ago, consulting a cunning man for a serious illness was not the first or the most desirable recourse; it was, however, believed to be a sure solution when dealing with dark witchery.

Once, there lived a woman in the countryside who was, by all accounts, of good health, but had suddenly taken to strange "fits." She would convulse at times, contorting her body, or would lose consciousness entirely. She seemed to have no control over herself in these moments, and afterwards, she would wake from her previous state with no knowledge of what had happened.

Doctors were consulted first, of course, in order to determine whether it be an illness known to man; alas, it was not. And so the fits continued, and the woman was left with little to think but that she was witched or cursed, marked by some malevolent practitioner for some unintended slight in the past, or perhaps simply marked for envy, a victim of the evil eye. For such things do happen.

At last, the woman consulted with a local wise man, often called a cunning man, who had some knowledge of witching ways and some manner of craft of his own, though his own magic was of the healing kind. He and his assistant paid a visit to the woman, assuring her that all would be well. While his man lit the fire, the cunning man gathered from the woman clippings of her fingernails and hair from her head, pronouncing strange prayers as he did so.

As he cast the hair and nail clippings upon the fire, a great shriek came forth from its flames, a terrible scream the likes of which could turn a man's blood backwards in his veins. It roared and bellowed all the way up the chimney, as if coming from the smoke itself. They could hear the scream passing up the chimney's length, then along the roof, with the chimney smoke, and they could hear it fade as it dispersed into the clear night sky.

After that night, the woman was never plagued by fits again, and all were sure that it had been witchery after all, and that the witch responsible had been harrowed by the counter-charm and forced to flee the area in fear, never to return. For those who deal in curses can always be served a dose of their own medicine, if one knows how.

A Cold Wind in Hell
Scotland

All over the Western isles of Scotland known as the Hebrides, witching folk were known to conjure storms at sea. One such warlock of note went by the name of MacVuirich, or Macpherson of Power, called *Mac-Mhuirich nam buadh* in the old Gaelic. His talent for conjuring gales was legendary, for he could make supplication to the winds much in the way some make petition to saints, and when he beckoned, they would rush across the sea to answer him.

It happened once that the sorcerer Macpherson, accompanied only by his beloved dog, was on a voyage from near South Uist, but it was an unusually calm day at sea, and there was little wind to speed the journey. The skipper, knowing the old warlock's reputation, expected that he would readily oblige to quicken their pace by conjuring a gale or summoning a wave to carry them, but he did not. This annoyed the skipper. What was the benefit, he thought, of having a reputed wizard on board if he would not fill their sails?

"Won't you do something, man? We're moving at a snail's pace. Call to your winds," said the skipper.

"Very well," said Macpherson, and so he spoke the following charm:

> *I call an East Wind from the aether calm,*
> *As the Lord of the Elements has ordained,*
> *A wind that needs not rowing nor reefing,*
> *That will do naught deceitful unto us.*

At that moment, a gentle wind flowed over the waves and filled the ship's sails, softly careening the vessel onward at a faster pace than before. This was no mighty gale, though, as the skipper had imagined, and he was disappointed. He had expected a great rushing force that would carry them at once across the water, and like a fool, he pressed Macpherson to do more.

"Is that all you can conjure?" said the skipper. "I'm the one at the helm, I suppose. Were it your own boat, perhaps you would give it your best instead of this weak and trifling charm-work of yours."

"Very well," said Macpherson, and so he spoke the second charm:

> *I call a North Wind hard as a rod,*
> *Struggling above our gunwale,*
> *Like a red roe sore pressed,*
> *Descending a hillock's narrow hard head.*

At that moment, a stronger wind rushed over the waves, and the boat rocked a bit, and the sails strained against the force filling them, pushing the boat speedily along the sea. This was a strong wind, for sure, but the skipper was still unsatisfied, for it would still take a bit of time for their journey at this pace, and he was ever a sour, discontented person. And so, like a fool, he pressed the warlock a third time, insulting him as he did so.

"Some power you have," said the skipper. "This wind may as well be nothing. A trifling bit of breath is all you can conjure, I suppose."

"Very well," said Macpherson gravely, his countenance growing dark with anger, and so he spoke the third charm:

> *If there be a cold wind in Hell,*
> *Devil, send it after us,*

In waves and surges,
And if one go ashore, let it be I,
And if two, I and my dog.

And at that moment, the sky grew dark, and the waves began to grow and crest something terrible, and thunder and lightning pealed across the sky, and the wind that rose was like a great rushing cry across the sea, as if the doors of Hell had opened somewhere in the ocean and all the miserable souls therein were screaming in agony, and the boat rocked violently until at last a giant wave arose, rolling along as if by the great and terrible arm of some ancient devil of the sea, and the whole boat was overturned, casting everyone aboard into the deep.

The tempest dispelled shortly afterwards, and the sky grew clear, and the water became calm again. And somewhere on the shoreline, the warlock Macpherson emerged from the waters, having been carried safely on a wave, and his dog walked onto the shore by his side. The warlock gazed upon the waters coldly with his gray eyes, and petted his dog on the head. Then the two went on their way, the old charmer and his loyal hound, continuing the next leg of their journey by foot, leaving the dead behind them in the sea.

The Charmer's Daughter
Isle of Man

There are some sorcerers of old, dear reader, who become so legendary in the course of their lives that they are remembered long after, and the tales and descriptions of these people pass into myth. This is the case of one charmer of the Teare family of Ballawhane, whose power of craft was so great as to become famous, and to establish a dynasty of charmers long after his death.

In the old accounts, Mr. Teare is variously described as a seer, a charmer, a witch-man, and a healer. He was of small stature, and he wore quite plain clothes, natural fibers undyed and of neutral colors. Nothing about the man was garish, and he was no showman of any kind, but his reputation on the isle spoke for itself. In hard times, when one's cattle took mysteriously ill, or when a curse could not be undone, or when one's home was plagued by spirits, or when death felt very near, old man Teare was the one to send for, if he was available, for he was much in-demand and was known as a charmer of charmers, a master of the old cunning.

Once, they say that a man in Laxey sought the craft of old man Teare, for his fields of grain were set upon by enormous flocks of sparrows, and without intervention, they were sure to bring his crop to ruin. And so Mr. Teare set off into the field, where he conducted the ritual necessary for the charm. When he returned to the man, he told him that, in the future, it would be best if he could charm the seed before it was sown so as to prevent this from happening again, but that the sparrows would not return this season. The man was in disbelief of this, and he suspected that he had perhaps been conned, as did several other farmers with whom he shared this tale. They eventually decided to watch the fields together to see what would happen, and surely enough, every field that was not charmed by Mr. Teare was set upon by the sparrows, but the charmed field was untouched, even though it lay just beside the others in close proximity.

And it is said that Teare's daughter was gifted with the same abilities after his death, for charmers on the Isle of Man were known to pass their powers from man to woman and from woman to man across the generations so that one practitioner's craft might live through the ages. The daughter of Teare was consulted often in matters of luck, especially by fishermen who were ever eager for her to charm their fishing nets and bless them with a great haul of fish.

Some say that she inherited old Teare's book of charms as well, containing his formulas and conjurations of protection, healing, and other arts mastered by him during his lifetime. And it may be true, even today, that one of the many Teare families of the Isle of Man keeps such a book, and passes its secrets of hereditary charming from one generation to the next, so preserving their traditions and the memory of beloved ancestors long gone—ancestors who healed and cared for their communities during their lifetimes—and whose power and wisdom live on in their children's children to this day.

Going By Night
New World

Long ago, how many years we cannot say for certain, in what is now an area in upstate New York, near Albany, there lived a small family. They had one daughter, and it happened one day that this girl began to experience strange events that horrified her, and her parents even more so.

On certain evenings, the girl could feel her spirit loosen from her body, which would come on quite suddenly and without warning, causing her to pass through walls and through locked windows and doors, as if she were made of ether. These sensations intensified over time and became so frequent that the girl was quite incapable of remaining in her body for long enough to do anything else. Eventually, and most often at night, she could feel herself flying above the countryside in the moonlit sky, untethered from her body, as if someone had cut the thread that tied her to her own flesh and bones.

It was then that the family summoned a conjurer, an expert in such matters as witchcraft and devilry, to help determine the exact cause and to find a solution. The man confirmed that this was indeed witchcraft, and that the witches desired to take the girl completely from them, whether by death or by initiation into those ways, we cannot say.

The conjurer gathered the entire family together in their old barn one dark night, and took the girl up into the hayloft above, and asked that the mother and father remain down below, for though they were welcome to listen on silently to what followed, he could not have them interfere or be seen when he summoned the dark spirit, lest his charms against those dread powers be broken.

And so the man began his incantations above by candlelight, and the mother and father heard only his voice pronouncing words they could not understand, and they could barely see anything in the barn except the glimmer of his faint lantern, which had been turned down quite low. Eventually, however, they saw a great shadow interrupt the lantern's soft light, and they heard a loud, slow creaking in the barn's loft, as if something large and heavy had settled and spread its weight there, straining the old boards of wood.

"This girl is not yours, and you must leave her be," said the conjurer in the darkness.

"We'll see," said a low and rumbling voice, which sounded nothing like a human woman or man at all.

"You've no choice. If you stay, I'll thrash you with my cat o' nine tails," said the man.

"We'll see," said the voice again, lower and slower than before.

"If you do not leave this girl in peace, I will use all of my powers against you, and you will be destroyed," said the man at last.

And the other voice was quiet for a long time, until at last it spoke, slowly and calmly. "Tomorrow," it said, "you will travel by the old crossroads, and there we shall meet face to face, and then, o man, we shall see."

What happened after that night is a strange affair indeed, and quite open to interpretation. For the girl claimed that her episodes of traveling had ceased after that, and the deep voice heard by the parents was never heard by them again. But the conjurer, who did indeed travel by the crossroads the next day—for he had another appointment to keep in a nearby town—was never seen or heard from again, and seemingly disappeared after that, never reaching his next destination. And to this day, one cannot say for certain whether the girl was saved from those dark powers, or whether she was brought into their number.

The Witch-Spelled Cow
Ireland

Somewhere near Dungannon, several generations ago, there lived two farmers who often sold and traded livestock, being old neighbors and generally good friends in their own way. They fell into disagreement, however, over a cow that had supposedly been bewitched, and once the one farmer filed lawsuit against the other, the two ended up before a judge, and the plaintiff was asked to convey the story of what had happened.

The plaintiff farmer said that he had purchased the cow from his neighbor, the defendant, at a fair price, for he knew at the time that it was "blinked," or had the evil eye upon it. No milk would she give, though she ate well and had no signs of ill health. The defendant, he said, had agreed to send for a wise woman or charmer who lived on a mountain nearby, and he promised that he would do all she said to restore the cow at no expense to him or his farm.

The wise woman's instructions were simple, but were to be followed strictly down to the very letter. First, she said to pull hair from the cow's forehead, from her back, from her tail, and from under her nostrils. Then, the defendant was to write the names of eight neighbors who were suspected of witchcraft against his farm, with the name of the most likely suspect written at the top of the list. Then he was to procure a piece of thatch from the roof of the chief suspect, which should be burned in a fire along with some sod, the hairs, and the paper with the names writ upon it. A clump of this charred sod was then to be held before the cow, and if all had been done correctly, and the cow licked the sod, the animal would be witched no more.

The judge, having sat through the plaintiff's long description of events, was clearly frustrated by the complexity of the case. "Well, did the cow lick the thing or not?" he asked, rubbing his forehead in vexation.

"Lick it? She would have ate it," replied the plaintiff, at which many in the courtroom laughed. "But that fool forgot to burn the thatch as the wise woman said, and so the cow succumbed to witchcraft after all."

A Sieve by Sea
Scotland

A very long time ago, on the Isle of Skye, there lived a husband and wife who were newlyweds. Their life was happy and generally unremarkable, save for the fact that the wife disappeared each night from their marriage bed, and did not return until morning. After several nights of this behavior, the husband attempted to follow her, but found that she was too quick or too clever, for the woman quite disappeared once she left their bedroom.

One night, finding he could no longer tolerate his wife's secrecy, the husband pretended to sleep in order to spy on her and find out where she was going each night and what business she was up to at such strange hours. He watched

silently as she rose from their bed, then spoke a strange
prayer which he had never heard, and was transformed into a
cat. He followed the cat, which wandered down the road a
ways, and made its way to a cliff's edge overlooking the sea.

There, on that craggy cliff, by the light of the moon, his
wife, who was surely a witch, joined a company of other cats,
a great throng of cats of all shapes and colors, a gathering of
all of the witches of Skye. "I go in the name of the Devil,"
spoke a male cat in a somber tone, and he took a sieve and
threw it upon the water, and then leapt down into it from an
impossible height, landing safely, and sailed over the silvery
waves.

One by one, each witch-cat in their congregation did the
same, casting their sieve upon the waves with the words, "I
go in the name of the Devil," then sailing off. At last, it was
his wife's turn to sail away, presumably towards their meeting
place where they would hold their great ceremonies of
witchery that night. For it is known that all witches are
summoned to take part in that hidden communion on certain
nights, traveling across the land and sea in a variety of forms.

Shocked by all that he had witnessed, and fearing for his
wife's body and soul, the man cried out, "Save us, O God,
in the name of the Father, Son, and Holy Ghost," and at
this, the charm was broken, and all of the witch-cats sank
into the sea, and presumably drowned. And one wonders what
crossed the man's mind then, as he gazed over the waves

searching for his wife, perhaps wishing he had allowed her to keep her secrets after all.

A Host of Spirits
England

Dealings with spirits, a subject which often made for the most wild and fantastical portions of the witch trials, were considered an important hallmark of witchcraft itself. The condemnation of this practice was almost always derived from the popular translation of the phrase "familiar spirits" in numerous portions of the King James Version of the bible, a phrase that refers historically to a variety of workings with spirits in the animistic magical practices of the ancient world. English witches, in particular, were always believed to keep familiar spirits, which could take many forms.

In the late 1600s, Alice Duke, an accused witch, was believed to keep a familiar spirit, which served her interests and aided her in all things, and this spirit took the form of a small cat. It was Alice's obligation, we are told in the trial documents, to feed the familiar by allowing it to suckle from her, and it was said that when the imp fed, it went into a sort of trance-like state.

The accused witch Mary Johnson was also believed to keep a familiar spirit in animal form, though hers was perhaps more strange. She was said to have as her servant a familiar that looked like a rat, but without ears or a tail. She was believed to carry this creature about with her in her pocket, where none could see it unless it chose to reveal itself.

Arthur Bill, a young man accused of witchcraft after his parents had suffered the same fate, was believed to keep three familiars about him. These bore the names of *Grissil*, *Ball*, and *Jack*. In folklore, we find the name *Jack* quite ubiquitous when it comes to spirits of pagan origin, so it is likely that poor Arthur gave his tormentors an answer that he knew they would accept.

Bess Horner, also in the late 1600s, was accused of witchcraft involving what has now become a classic trope of the modern image of the witch: a familiar in the form of a toad. Bess was believed to feed her familiar by allowing it to suckle from a teat that was also her "witch-mark," given by the Devil himself.

In the early 1700s, Jane Wenham, the famous Witch of Walkern, was believed to employ imps or familiar spirits in a very unique fashion. Jane was, of course, one of the very last witches to be executed in England. Her accusers claimed that she had sent dozens of familiars to torment them, all resembling cats, except for one important detail: every cat had the face of the witch who sent them. They claimed that these identical cats with her own human face on them would plague their doorstep at all hours, by day and night.

The Fork-Stuck Sieve
New World

Long ago, somewhere near Salisbury, Maryland, there lived a young bachelor who was tormented each night. No sooner did he fall asleep in his bed than he would be visited by a great black cat of enormous size, with cruel, glowing eyes. It would leap onto his bed and rest on his chest, and the weight of it was greater than any earthly cat, such that it would pin him in place and strain his breathing. And all the while, it would simply stare into his eyes silently until morning came, at which point it would vanish.

This went on for a long time, and the young man was so full of dread each night that he hardly slept at all anymore. And it was a long while before he asked for help, for who would believe such a thing? He tried bolting the windows and sealing up the fireplace, hoping to prevent the cat's arrival each night, but nothing worked, and at last he conceded that this must be a witch in the form of a black cat, a shape many witches are known to take by night.

Eventually, the young man grew so desperate that he sought out the aid of a conjure woman who lived nearby, for she knew a thing or two about the ways of witches. She knew which parts of the bible could be used for spells against harm, and she knew how to dress candles with oils in the old conjure ways, and every Black family for miles around had at least one story about the woman's strange powers.

"If the cat truly be a witch," said the conjure woman, "then she won't stop until she is punished. Take a sieve, and stick the prongs of a fork through it, then set it upside-down beside your bed so that the prongs stick up through the bottom."

This seemed strange to the young bachelor, but he decided it was best not to argue, and so he followed the conjure woman's instructions, setting the fork-stuck sieve on the table beside his bed. That night, as the black cat came to harass him once more, it leapt up onto the table, and was stuck by the prongs sticking through the sieve. The creature yowled and screeched something dreadful, for the charm's magic held it in place like glue, and it could not get away.

"I'll release you now, witch," said the young man, "on the condition that you never enter this home again so long as you live," to which the cat blinked in agreement. As soon as he pulled the sieve out from under it, the cat hissed at him one final time, then went on its way, vanishing into the darkness, and he never did see the thing again.

Strangely enough, though, a woman of the neighborhood was said to have taken to bed the very next day, suffering from sharp pains in her chest, as if pricked by a fork.

The Black Goat
Ireland

Many ages ago, during the horror and cruelty of the witch hunts, there lived a poor old woman near Antrim. She was believed by many to be a witch and a practitioner of dark arts, and though legend does not speak to her witchery, it does speak to the events of her death, and to the curse that followed.

It came to pass that, over time, as the people grew more and more afraid of witches, this particular old woman was harassed and threatened by night and by day, such that she had not a single friend in the village and was eventually driven quite mad by her suffering. And so she sought refuge in an old cave in order to escape her tormentors. Unfortunately for her, choosing an old cave for a dwelling only confirmed, in the eyes of the fear-maddened townspeople, that she was, in fact, a witch of the evil sort, and people being what they are, they set out one night to murder her.

She was stabbed to death, they say, in that very cave, and her killing was coordinated by none other than a sexton by the name of MacGregor. Her body was cut into pieces, and the ashes of these burnt pieces were scattered over all of the homes and farms she was believed to have cursed with her witchery.

But this was not the end of the matter by any means, for the cave in which she dwelled, and where her murder took place, was connected via tunnels to the old town meeting house where the sexton looked after the churchyard. And so, for many years after, the spirit of the accused witch was seen to roam about as a black goat, haunting the sexton's footsteps night and day, and terrifying anyone who came near.

And perhaps, in the end, the people did realize that it was the sexton MacGregor who was the true monster, for the apparition of the black goat was named "MacGregor's ghost," the apparition being a spirit of vengeance and wrath conjured as a result of his own malice, after all.

The Lock Charm
Scotland

There lived once, long ago, though not so long as some might imagine, a man on the Isle of Skye by the name of Archibald, who was popularly known as Archibald the Light-Headed, or *Gilleasbuig Aotrom*. He was so-named, they say, due to his madness, by which he got himself into all sorts of foolish trouble. But he was also an accomplished sorcerer, and he was quite famous for his possession of a particular charm called the lock charm, which could open all barred or locked gates, and would silence any dogs that attempted to prevent his entry to any property whatsoever.

Though Archibald was said to have been blessed with wit and eloquence of speech, his madness made him quite unpredictable, and this, coupled with his powers as a dark sorcerer, made him a feared figure indeed. His nature was capricious, a charmer who could either help or harm, as he willed, and so it was always wise to tread carefully around him so as to give no offense. It is said that anywhere he went, dogs would cower and whimper, going into other rooms or hiding under furniture in order to avoid his gaze, either due to his use of the charm itself, or due to animals' abilities to sense both madness and dark sorcery around them.

It is believed by some that the lock charm used by old Archibald was sourced in a particular passage of the Old Testament related to the escape of the Hebrews from Egypt, which makes it much like many other Scottish charms of the era, for it was common practice that anything biblical or liturgical be adapted into new forms in the old craft—and put towards a variety of ends. The charm was pronounced out loud so quickly, however, that none could hear it well enough to remember it, and thus, although Archibald used the charm as he pleased, none were able to acquire it from him during his lifetime. And today, it is lost—or so they say.

The Bloodied Milk
Isle of Man

Along the coastal countryside near Castletown, there once lived a farmer whose cow had developed a strange condition. The poor cow's udders would give only bloodied milk, and though all of the usual treatments were tried, none sufficed, and day after day, more blood would come, until at last it was determined that the cow must be bewitched, for it was known in those days that any farm too prosperous, or any family too proud, could suffer the witch's evil eye, and so their prosperity would be "ill-willed," or cursed.

Finally, the farmer sent for a charm-man, for this particular man was something of a white witch and knew what procedures to use to reverse such curses. The charmer gave the man some dried herbs in a packet and imparted the instructions for their use. He was to set the bloody milk to boiling over his hearth, then stir the herbs into the same pot. Most importantly, he was told not to abandon his post over the cooking pot, no matter what he heard or saw, but to hold firm and show courage.

The man did as he was told that night, setting the bloody milk to boil, then stirring in the herbs. It was not long after he commenced this that he heard a violent knocking on the door, which began slowly, then became faster and louder until it reached a feverish pace. The cows of the farm cried out in the darkness outside, as if something strange had terrified them. Most disturbingly, stones began falling down the chimney into his hearth, dropping into the boiling pot, and splashing its hot contents about. The poor farmer, disturbed by all of this, abandoned his post by the hearth and ran to hide in his bedroom, at which all of the commotion ceased.

The next day, the cow gave bloody milk yet again, and so the farmer set out to return to the charm-man once more. He confessed the truth of the night before, that he had not shown courage, but was filled with fear at the strange knocking and the lowing of the cows, and most of all at the stones falling from the chimney. The charmer assured him that all would be well, but he must do the thing again, and this time, he must not leave the hearthside, no matter what may happen.

The following night, he commenced the ritual again, following all of the instructions as before: boiling the bloody milk, then setting the herbs therein. As he stirred the pot, the same commotion began. The cows cried out, and there was a loud knocking at the door, and stones began to tumble down the chimney. This time, however, he did not run and hide, but held firm.

The phenomena grew louder and more violent, and eventually, the little windows of the house began creaking, as if under pressure to burst inward, and at last, one of the windows burst clean through, sending glass flying everywhere, and there on his own floor, among the broken shards of glass, lay the witch, who had tumbled through the ruined window quite against his will. The witch-man begged the farmer then, pleading with him to forgive him and to take the pot off the fire, for it pained him so, and he swore that he would never bewitch his farm again for the rest of his days. And the witch kept this promise, it seems, for the farmer had no need to consult the charm-man a third time.

The Bell Witch
New World

Several generations ago, in northwest Tennessee, there lived a wealthy family of the surname Bell, who owned a great deal of land and made their home along the Red River. It was during the purchase of one particular piece of land from the Batts family, they say, that John Bell made an egregious error. Having previously agreed to buy the land from Kate Batts for a fair price, he then went back on his word at the time of sale, refusing to pay the agreed sum and offering her only a meager portion of what the land was worth. At this, she was greatly angered, for it was too late for her to back out of the deal, and she had no choice but to accept far less than she was owed.

Now, this offense may have seemed small to a man as well-to-do as John Bell, for the very rich rarely become so except by way of callousness, but the rumor among many was that old Kate Batts was a witch. She was known to keep strange ways and customs, and it was said that she asked for a brass pin from every woman she met so that she might use them in her witchcraft, and by such means hold power over the families of the area. Many were those who believed Kate Batts to be a witch of the dark sort, practicing black magic and conjuring wicked spirits to punish those who offended her. And Kate never forgave John Bell for the crooked deal, for the Batts family fell into debt and suffered greatly as a result, and it is said that on her deathbed, she promised ominously that she would have her vengeance on the Bell family yet.

Surely enough, in the years that followed, strange events did indeed begin to manifest around the Bell property. John Bell, while walking through his own cornfields, was confronted by a strange animal that appeared to have the body of a great hound and the head of a rabbit. It stared menacingly at him until he mustered the courage to fire his rifle at it, at which point it disappeared into the tall rows of corn.

Soon after that, his son, Drew Bell, suffered a strange encounter of his own. He was walking along the property when he came across a large bird, which he imagined to be a turkey. He ran inside the house to fetch his gun, then returned to the spot, thinking he might shoot it for supper, but as he approached, he realized that this was no turkey at all, but an enormous bird the likes of which he had never seen. When he came close, it flapped its tremendous wings, which terrified him, and flew away.

Betsy Bell, the young daughter of the family, was to have her own encounter with the forces at work around them. Walking along the edge of the forest that bordered the Bell house, the girl saw something strange: it appeared to be another little girl, much like herself, but dressed in green. It swung from the low-hanging limb of an enormous oak tree, staring at her all the while.

Others who frequented the property reported strange sightings of their own. A spectral rabbit or "hare ghost" was seen running about the grounds, which could not be shot or caught, but would disappear. A great black dog was said to prowl around the land along a particular path, stopping at the same place every day at the exact same time, as if following precise instructions in its patrol.

And it was not long after these appearances that the spirit began speaking to the family in their own home, announcing itself variously under a variety of names, including Cypocryphy, Blackdog, Mathematics, Jerusalem, and Kate. The latter of which was its favorite name, and the name to which it was most likely to respond when addressed. Nor did the Bell Witch, as folks took to calling it, seem to have a single personality or character, but seemed to vary in its affectations and behavior over time, as if the entity were, in fact, a host of spirits sent to torment them. These voices could sing, recite the bible, hurl insults, or speak in a gentle, mocking sweetness.

The family was most terrified, however, of the physical manifestations, for when the Bell Witch was in a certain mood, objects would fly from shelves, sheets would be ripped off of beds in the dead of night, and members of the family would be physically grabbed, pushed, and assaulted. These events went on for years, until the Bell family became infamous for being cursed, to such an extent that the family was paid a visit by future president Andrew Jackson, who was interested in seeing the phenomenon for himself, but fled the house in fear, saying quite famously that he would prefer to fight the British again than face the Bell Witch.

Over the course of years, the Bell family consulted a variety of witching men, wise women, herb doctors, conjure folk, and even psychic mediums in their attempts to banish the spirit. This series of rituals and seances brought no remedy, however, but seemed only to empower the entity further. At one time, the Bell Witch told them that its true identity was that of a tortured soul who simply wanted its remains buried so that it could be laid to rest. After witnesses searched under the house, the entity laughed, confessing that the entire story was a lie. Another time, the Bell Witch told an audience at the house that it was the ghost of an early settler, and that it could not rest until someone found its buried treasure. After watching them seek the supposed treasure for some time, the spirit laughed once more at this manipulation, and confessed that this was another lie.

Eventually, the family came to realize that no manner of approach could convince the Bell Witch to leave them be. The daughter, Betsy, was forced to break off an engagement to a young man as a result of the spirit's persecution, and John Bell grew ill and feeble over many years of living in this state of torment, and eventually died. There are rumors, to this day, that the Bell Witch had somehow poisoned his food in order to bring about his death, but this seems uncharacteristically merciful for a host of spirits so focused on prolonged suffering.

Some say that the spirits conjured by the witch gave their greatest performance at the funeral of John Bell, for as the family gathered to mourn their patriarch, the event was interrupted by the many voices of the entity known as the Bell Witch, singing bawdy pub songs loudly and drunkenly, as if celebrating the death of John Bell and mocking all who had gathered to mourn him.

The Catching Gaze
Ireland

It was long ago, somewhere on the Aran Islands, that a man sought the services of a so-called *cailleach*, or wise woman, in order to find treatment for an incurable disease. No doctor could offer him any treatment at all, they say, and so the man was forced to turn to unconventional means, despite the fact that this particular wise woman was rumored to be a witch, capable of craft far darker than the usual healing charms and remedies.

The woman assessed his condition, and she agreed to help for a small fee, but her methods for curing this particular malady were dark indeed. She told him that she could draw the sickness from him, but that it must be passed to another, and so, after pulling his sickness into herself, she must go out near a public road in search of a particular herb. Upon finding it, she would drop down to her knees while employing certain incantations, then pluck the plant, looking up as she did so. The first stranger on whom she set her glance was sure to take on the disease themselves, and would die from it.

The man agreed to this course of treatment, and we should be careful not to judge him for it. Who can say with certainty what one might agree to when death knocks upon our door? At any rate, it is not known whether the man fully recovered, or if some stranger—or worse, someone he knew—died as a result of his choice, buying him more years of life at the cost of their own. But of course, if such a charm did yield such results, one would not announce it publicly, would they?

Two Rats at Sea
Scotland

Once, off the western coast of Scotland, a very long time ago, there lived a merchant boatman who ferried loads of peat and other goods across the waters so as to sell them and earn his living. On one gray day, he was making his way across the waves with his load of goods, when he spied something strange just off the side of his boat.

He had perhaps thought that one of his parcels had fallen into the water and was floating there, but this was not the case. Sailing beside his own boat was a much smaller one, just off to the side and down in the water, made from strange materials of hair and dirt and bits of dried dung. And aboard this small vessel were two rats, who stood perfectly still with their noses to the wind, and the vessel sailed forward in a straight line, as if drawn along by some invisible hand.

Now, it is well-known that such encounters with spirits demand careful etiquette. One never knows what harm may come if offense is given, for whatever reason, particularly when such spirits are minding their own business and bothering no one at all. But such wisdom was apparently lost on the boatman, for he took a handful of peat from the load of his boat, and he cast it at the two rats aboard their vessel. Their ship, being made of such fragile stuff, broke apart immediately, and the two rodents sank into the sea and drowned.

Shortly after, however, the boatman realized his egregious mistake, for a great storm arose over the waters, and the sky grew dark and roiling. The waves began to grow and rise, and thunder rang out, shaking the air, and lightning pealed across the sky. The wind that whipped his little boat set a terrible fear upon him, and he was sure then that the two rats had been witches in their spirit forms, and that he had angered them beyond all forgiveness, and that he was sure to die that day as a result of his actions.

The boatman strained his sails against the wind, and used every ounce of his wits and his strength to guide the vessel, and somehow, by only the skin of his teeth, made his way to shore, though his haul of wares was quite lost in the process. And from that day forward, he took greater care when encountering spirits at sea.

A Coat of Clay
England

A great many ages ago, in the countryside of Lincolnshire, there lived a wise woman who was known throughout those parts for her knowledge and her remedies. She was consulted often, and she earned her living by treating aches and pains, curing diseases in cattle, and divining whether one's sweetheart would be true. Some called her a witch, but only in secret, for she did not like to be called such, and she was ever of a foul temper and suffered no fools on her doorstep.

One day, as she sat on her stoop peeling potatoes, there came to her door a young man. "Good morning, witch," he announced with an idiot's smile. "I've come to seek your guidance in a very important matter."

The wise woman groaned in response, mumbling something under her breath, but did not look up.

"Did you hear me, witch? I'm in need of your help with something important."

"I heard a fool. And I see a fool before me," said the wise woman, loudly and clearly this time. "Get on with it, then. What do you want?"

"But that's it exactly," said the young man. "You must truly be a witch, for you've already guessed. My mother, my father, and everyone in the town believe me stupid, and I must know how to prove them wrong."

The wise woman looked at the young man, puzzled, and then broke into a riotous laughter. "Until you find yourself a coat of clay, a fool you shall remain. Now off with you."

And so the young man went on his way, and as he passed along the roadside, he came across a length of muddy track that sucked at his shoes. *This be the witch's prophecy*, thought the young man, and so he rolled in the mud until he was coated in the stuff, and he thought himself well on the way to being wise, for this must surely be the "coat of clay" the witch mentioned.

As he continued on his way back to town, he came across a young woman in the street with lovely curls and a pretty face. "Can I call on you sometime?" asked the young man, covered in mud, "for I shall soon be a wise man, and my future is bright."

"Of course," said the young woman. "What girl can resist a fool covered in mud?" And then she went on her way, and the young man thought to himself that this was perhaps not the coat of clay that the witch meant after all.

He then decided to plunge himself into a river nearby, if only to remove the mud. And so he walked on, soaking wet, until he came across a patch of dusty road, dry as a bone. *Perhaps this be the witch's prophecy*, he thought, and so he rolled around in the dust, and his wet clothes were quite covered, and he thought himself well on the way to being wise.

It was then that a merchant passed by with his horse and cart, and the young man, who was once again covered in filth, had to roll quickly out of the way to avoid being crushed. "Fool boy!" cried the merchant as he rode past, and the young man thought to himself that this was perhaps not the coat of clay that the witch meant after all.

He came at last to a tavern, and decided to stop in for a drink. He sat himself down, and the owner happened by, finding the young man covered in filth and looking quite glum. "What's wrong with you, boy? Are you quite all right?" he asked.

"No, sir," said the young man. "I've done everything I can think of to get myself a coat of clay, so I can be wise like the witch told me, but nothing seems to work."

"Have a drink, boy," said the man. "And after you've drunk enough, you'll surely find your coat of clay, whatever that be."

And so the young man proceeded to get very drunk, and when he stood up, the room spun round, and he felt better, but he still had no idea how to find the right coat of clay. What's more, he had no money and was unable to pay for his drinks, which earned him a good kick out the door and several harsh words from the tavern man.

Deciding to return to the wise woman for clarity, the young man made his way back down the road, arriving on her doorstep at last to find her sitting and smoking her pipe. Upon seeing the young man, who was drunk and covered in dirt, bruised from his treatment at the tavern, she fell into a riotous laughter once more, coughing great plumes of smoke from her pipe and nearly falling over in her amusement.

"Please tell me, at last," pleaded the fool, "how am I ever to find the right coat of clay?"

"Coat of clay?" echoed the woman, raising one eyebrow.

"Yes, you told me before that I would remain a fool until I found myself a coat of clay."

And the wise woman broke into laughter once more, holding her belly and weeping. "You stupid boy," she said at last, her voice still cracking with amusement. "When you're dead and buried deep in the ground, then you'll have your coat of clay. And in a hundred years or more, when none living can remember your stupidity, then you'll be a fool no more."

The Witch's Stone
Scotland

Long ago, on the Isle of Barra, there lived a very famous witch who was gifted in the giving of portents, prophecies, and divinations. Her auguries were sought out by merchants, seamen, and young women all, for her powers were supposed to be particularly accurate and reliable, and by such craft, she earned enough money to make her living.

Young women seeking husbands would come to her in order to ask about their sweethearts, to find out whether they would be true, and to find out what sort of life they might expect should they accept a marriage proposal, for in those days, a young woman's choice of husband was a serious matter indeed, being the main determiner of her quality of life for the rest of her days—or the lack thereof. Merchants and sailors of all kinds would visit the seer-witch of Barra in order to attain knowledge that would help them in their dealings, in choosing this deal or another, or in knowing where to fish or where to procure goods for the best price.

And they say that all of the woman's prophecies were achieved similarly, by means of a magical stone that was called the *Clach na Leigheas*, or stone of healing. It was a holed stone, or holey stone, the kind of stone formed when water runs through it over many years, forming a hole, which is a naturally occurring talisman of many legendary uses, but in this case, it had one in particular. They say that the witch could put her tongue through its hole, which imparted some magical quality to her speech, and afterwards, she could speak truths unknown to her, and those yet to come.

A Witch-Cat
New World

A great long while ago, somewhere in the lush pastures and warm fields of the American South, there lived a miller and his wife. By day, the man would work at his windmill, inspecting its millstone and tending to its rotors, and overseeing the work of milling grain for local farmers, from which he earned a modest living.

By night, however, the man was forced to flee the old mill, for strange things would happen each time he tried to work past sundown. Shadows could be seen moving about inside the mill, whispers could be heard, which would grow louder and louder until they became screams, and more than once, he felt an invisible hand grab him. After this happened several times, the miller refused to stay after dark, which was a defeat in his eyes, for it cut short his production and slowed down his progress in his work.

Eventually, there came a traveler to the door of the man and his wife, seeking shelter and rest from the road, and though he had no money, the man said that in exchange for food and rest, he would offer to do any work that needed doing about the mill.

"If you would stay with us," the miller said to the traveler, "I'll offer you my mill by night, for I am in great need of someone to stay there after dark and tell me what they see. But I must warn you first, before you agree." And so the miller told the traveler about the strange goings-on in the mill and how he himself was too frightened to stay there by night, how he only wanted someone else to bear witness and report back, so as to confirm that it was all real. To his surprise, the stranger agreed, and so they fed him and bid him good night and good luck.

The traveler made his way to the old mill then, and he set himself up in a corner, reclining against some old wood, pleased to have a dry and comfortable place to rest and food in his stomach. Beside him, he lay his small pocket bible and his knife, for these two treasures he always kept nearby. He then dozed off to sleep, thinking the miller must be a very frail man indeed, to be scared of nothing but shadows.

It was late in the evening, or perhaps the very early morning, when the man was woken abruptly by strange sounds, as if something were pacing about in the pitch-black mill. Somewhere perched above him, he could see a pair of glowing eyes staring down, and then another, and then another, until he counted nine pairs altogether.

At last, a dark cloud passed out of the moon's path, and by that pale light, he was able to see nine great cats all about him, enormous in size. These were no ordinary felines, but were surely witch-cats, the forms of witches when they travel about outside their own skins. One of the witch-cats leapt forward then and swiped at him, and the man instinctively reached for his knife and lashed out, and then all of the cats yowled in anger and fled into the night. The man sat awake, on guard inside the dark mill the entire night, for no sleep was possible after what he had just seen.

The next morning, the stranger found a little gold ring where he had struck the cat with the knife. He put it in his pocket, then walked back to the house in order to take breakfast with his hosts, but only the miller was there. Upon asking where the man's wife had gone, the miller replied that she was not feeling well, for her hand had slipped with a knife, and she had cut herself badly. The stranger then held out the little gold ring dropped by the witch-cat the night before, and the miller's eyes grew wide then, for this was his own wife's wedding ring.

The Hole Stone
Scotland

In another age, on the Isle of Coll, there once stood a large stone which was known by the locals for its healing and protective powers, called the *Clach Thuill*, or Hole Stone. Many would travel to visit the stone in times of great need and suffering, and if the old lore be believed, there was one specific charm which would be performed there, which may have been overseen by a dedicated cunning woman, skilly man, white witch, or other practitioner of the charming arts.

It was said that those who sought the benefit of the stone's power, which was especially efficacious against disease, were to be guided through the hole in the stone, which would have been large enough to accommodate a person of average size. This was to be done three times, all while reciting specific prayers. Each time the person passed through the stone, they were to take with them a small piece of meat in their hand, leaving some on the stone behind them as they went through.

If a gull or other sea-bird were to come and eat the pieces of meat left by the person, then it was said that the affliction had been "consumed" by that bird, and would pass on to it. The bird would then waste away afterwards, and the person who left the meat would be cured and protected, or so they say.

The Devil's Bride
New World

It is said that the Devil did take a bride once, many ages ago. The girl lived with her mother in Louisiana, and she was admired by many eligible young bachelors. Suitors came from miles around to court her, but after each visit, she would say to her mother, "Not this one, no. Why are all men so dull and tiresome?" Her mother grew weary of trying to find a match for her daughter, and we must understand that, in those days, for a girl to refuse to take a husband was considered an unfortunate matter indeed. Each time she refused another suitor, her mother grew more and more frustrated.

One day, her mother announced that she would host a contest of skill. She would take the largest pumpkin from their pumpkin patch, and have it strung by rope upon the highest bough of an old honey locust tree, which is a tree covered with sharp thorns. Whichever young bachelor could climb the tree and retrieve the pumpkin would have the girl's hand in marriage, she said, and though the girl protested with all her might, her mother could not be moved on this.

And so the contest was announced, and many young bachelors arrived, all confident in their skill, all full of pompous pride, all wearing garish clothes and strutting about the place like peacocks, but none were able to climb the thorny old tree to retrieve the pumpkin. At last, there arrived one exceedingly handsome young man. He had come on a carriage pulled by fine black horses, and he wore the finest fashions of the day, and as nimbly as you please, he climbed the thorny old honey locust tree in but a moment, and landed safely on the ground with the pumpkin in hand.

The young man asked to walk and talk with the girl who would be his bride, and as they strolled under the mossy oaks, taking in the last of the warm air under the setting sun, the young woman found herself completely under his spell. He took her hand in his, and his touch was both cold and hot at once, which was strange, but here was something about the way he held her hand—so gently, but with such confidence. And there was something about his eyes, so deep and black and beckoning. In that moment, she felt glad of the whole ordeal, for it had led her at last to a man she desired for her husband.

The girl's mother was, of course, overjoyed. She packed some of her daughter's things—those that weren't too worn or old—and gave the horses water for the long journey to come. "Will you take your old white mare?" the mother asked her daughter. "She loves you more than any other. I doubt anyone else could ride her. Though she is old, she is healthy and strong, and her coat is white as the moon."

"I'm sure I shall have finer horses at my new home," said the young woman.

And with that, the two departed, and not one sad thought of home crossed the girl's mind, only eagerness for the future and a burning passion for the new love of her life, the dark and mysterious stranger who had stolen her heart in one day. They eloped that very evening, and immediately they made their way to his estate, which he assured her was a great and glorious house.

Along the road, strange things happened. First came a black cat, which jumped and landed on the carriage beside the happy couple. It spoke quite clearly to the young man, saying, "Master, as we agreed, please return my jacket to me."

"But of course, little one," said the young man. "A deal well-struck." And so the groom took off his handsome jacket and gave it to the cat, which instantly became an imp with horns and a tail. It trotted off on its two hooves into the dark forest beside the road. The young bride gasped with fear, but her husband reassured her that all would be well.

Next came a black goat, which caught up with the carriage and spoke quite clearly in a deep tone: "Master, as we agreed, please return my shoes to me."

"But of course, little one," said the young man. "A deal well-struck." And so the young man cast his shoes off the side of the carriage, and after slipping two hooves into them, the black goat became another imp with a long beard and yellow eyes. Like the first, it ran off into the dark forest. The young bride was visibly shaken by this, but again, the young man reassured her that she had nothing to fear.

Then came a serpent, which fell upon the young man's lap from an overhanging tree branch. "Master," the serpent hissed, "please return my horses to me, as we agreed in our bargain."

"But of course, little one," said the young man. "A deal well-struck." And so he tossed the serpent onto the back of one of the beautiful black horses, and in an instant, the serpent became an imp once again, just like the others, this one with long, spindly arms and a winding, wagging tongue. It unhitched the two horses and rode away with them into the trees.

"How is this possible?" the young bride cried. "I took you for a man of finery and of fashion, but neither your jacket, nor your shoes, nor even your horses were your own. I fear I have married a vagabond, and now we have not even horses to draw our carriage."

"Have we not?" the young man replied with a smirk. "Step out of the carriage, and take a closer look. I think you'll find that there is still one horse left." The bride stepped to the front of the carriage, finding nothing there at all, but before she could speak a word, she was transformed into a horse herself. In her horror, she attempted to flee, but he was too swift, and hitched her to the carriage before she could resist. "And now, you will take us home," her husband commanded gravely.

It was a long journey, but somehow, the young bride was not fatigued from the road, only appalled at this cruel treatment. It was clear to her, at this point, that she had married the Devil himself. When they arrived at his home, the King of Hell removed her bridle, and she was transformed back into her old self, perhaps a bit worse for wear, but unharmed.

"You tricked me," said the young bride. "You are the very Devil, and disguised yourself by some black art."

"I only allowed you to fool yourself," said the Devil. "I told you no lies." And with that, he escorted her to what was to be her new home, which was indeed a great and stately house. The Devil left her then to attend to the management of Hell, and the young bride was left to her own devices.

The sun had risen again after the long night, and she strolled the grounds of the estate, weeping pitifully and filled with rage and regret at her situation. In the Deep South, when rain falls as the sun is shining, it is still said that the Devil's wife is crying. Who knows how long she strolled the properties of Hell, dropping tears along her path? Perhaps time in Hell is different from time on Earth. Perhaps those tears she left will be forever falling, eventually making their way to earth over the years. But I digress.

She came at last to a great garden in Hell's palace, and an old woman called out to her from a bench beside the blooming flowers. "Why do you weep so, child?" she asked. "There is no finer place to be than here, just on the edge of Hell, shielded from all that suffering, yet far from all that dreadful singing in heaven and toiling on the earth."

"I weep because I married the Devil. He did not tell me who he was until after I made my vows."

The old woman furrowed her brow. "I'll beat that boy for treating a young lady in such a way." She placed her arm around the bride to comfort her. "There, there, child. He's cunning, yes, but not half as cunning as I raised him to be. And if you are his bride, then I'm now your mother as well, and no harm shall come to you if you do as I say."

The young bride ceased her crying then and felt a bit better, for it was the first kind word anyone had spoken to her since she arrived in Hell.

"Now listen carefully. My son will return soon from his throne room, and he will try to turn you again into a mare, that he might show off his new horse before the aristocracy of Hell." The old woman rolled her eyes. "Such a showman. In any case, you must be ready for him. Go to the henhouse, and gather three eggs, but mind you, only take the filthy ones. Repeat back, now. Which ones are you to take?"

"Only three, and only the filthy ones."

"Clever girl. You don't want to know what happened to the last girl who took one of my clean eggs. Now, when he approaches you, refuse him three times, and each time, cast one of the eggs at his feet."

"You've helped me so much," said the bride, "but I do not even know your name."

"There are too many," said the old Dame of Hell. "Not even I can remember them all."

And not an hour later, just as the old woman had predicted, the Devil returned to his fine house and approached the young woman, who was sitting in the courtyard, three filthy eggs in hand.

"There's my beautiful new horse," he said. "Come, so that I might show you off to the proud courtiers of Hell."

"You'll do no such thing," she said. "Not on this day or any other. I refuse you, and I renounce your claim over me."

The Devil's eyes grew wide and fearsome, glowing from within. He began to run towards her, but she quickly threw one of the eggs upon the ground. As it cracked, a great plume of smoke rose up between them, and the smoke became a mist, and from the mist grew a great river, loud and rushing. Somewhere in the sound of that water, she could hear the old woman cackling in amusement.

But the Devil dove into the river nonetheless, and began swimming. The bride ran as quickly as her legs could carry her, and just as the Devil emerged on the other side, she cried out again, "I refuse you, and I renounce your claim over me!" And then she cast the second egg. Again rose a great plume of smoke, and the smoke became a great darkness, and that darkness became a dense thicket of briar. Again, she could hear the cackling of the old woman, who had surely fallen out of her chair laughing at her son's predicament.

But the Devil blew on a length of briar, and it began to smolder, and then the entire thicket began to burn, and he made his way through the flames. The bride ran once more, and just as the Devil came out the other side of the burning thicket, she tossed the final egg. "I refuse you, and I renounce you!" she cried out. "Give me back my freedom!"

And with that, another great plume of smoke emerged from the final egg, and the smoke became a pale light, and that light swelled until it became the moon, and the moon became her old white horse, the one she had discarded when she left her mother's house. The horse spoke, but it was the old woman's voice that came from the animal's mouth. "Home now, child. Quickly," it said. And with that, she climbed onto the horse's back. It kicked the Devil hard and rode away, and it did not stop until they reached home.

And so the Devil's bride returned to her own life, just as before, though she was surely changed. She was still, some would say, married to the King of Hell. Perhaps her husband was humbled by her cunning tricks. Perhaps that hard kick from her old horse softened him up a bit. Perhaps the girl was even able to visit with her mother-in-law in Hell from time to time, for the old woman would surely allow no harm to come to her. What we can say with some certainty is that the girl was grateful for her freedom after that day, grateful for her old white mare, and for her own home and her own things, however used and worn. She never married again, and eventually inherited her family's property, and was most content to be the ruler of her own affairs.

Bibliography

Ballads Weird and Wonderful. (1912). John Lane & Co.

Baring-Gould, S. (1897). *Curious Myths of the Middle Ages.* Longmans, Green, & Co.

Bergen, F. D. (1899). "Two Negro Witch Stories." *The Journal of American Folklore,* 12(45), pp. 145-146.

Bottrell, W. (1873). *Traditions and Hearthside Stories of West Cornwall.* Beare and Son.

Bottrell, W. (1880). *Stories and Folk-Lore of West Cornwall.* F. Rodda.

Campbell, J. G. (1900). *Superstitions of the Highlands and Islands of Scotland.* James MacLehose and Sons.

Campbell, J. G. (1902). *Witchcraft and the Second Sight in the Highlands and Islands of Scotland: Tales and Traditions Collected Entirely from Oral Sources.* J. MacLehose and Sons.

Childs, A. (1929). "The Red Bag Under the Churn: A Folktale of the Kentucky Mountains." *American Speech,* 5(2), pp. 142-144.

Colles, A. (1887). "A Witches' Ladder." *The Folk-Lore Journal,* 5, pp. 1-5.

Cox, J. H. (1943). "The Witch Bridle." *Southern Folklore Quarterly,* 7(4), pp. 204-209.

Cross, T. P. (1919). "Witchcraft in North Carolina." *Studies in Philology,* 16(3), pp. 217-287.

Currier, J. M. (1891). "Contributions to New England Folklore." *The Journal of American Folklore*, 4(14), pp. 253-256.

Davis. M. E. M. (1905). "De Witch-'Ooman an' de Spinnin'-Wheel: The Witch Prevented from Re-Entering Her Skin: A Tale from Louisiana." *The Journal of American Folklore*, 18(70), pp. 251-252.

Douglas, G. (1901). Scottish Fairy and Folk Tales. Walter Scott.

Emerson, P. H. (1894). *Welsh Fairy Tales and Other Stories*. D. Nutt.

Fortier, A. (1895). *Louisiana Folk-Tales: In French Dialect and English Translation*. American Folk-Lore Society.

Gardner, E. E. (1914). "Folk-Lore from Schoharie County, New York." *The Journal of American Folklore*, 27(105), pp. 304-325.

Grierson, E. W. (1918). *The Scottish Fairy Book*. T. F. Unwin.

Hartland, E. S. (1892). County Folklore: Printed Extracts from Gloucestershire. The Folk-Lore Society.

Hunt, R. (1903). *Popular Romances of the West of England: The Drolls, Traditions, and Superstitions of Old Cornwall*. Chatto & Windus.

Ingram, M. V. (1894). *An Authenticated History of the Famous Bell Witch: The Wonder of the 19th Century,* and Unexplained Phenomenon of the Christian Era. Setliff, & Co.

Jacobs, J. (1892). *Celtic Fairy Tales*. David Nutt.

Jacobs, J. (1894). *More English Fairy Tales*. D. Nutt.

Linton, E. L. (1861). *Witch Stories*. Chapman and Hall.

MacManus, S. (1904). *In Chimney Corners: Merry Tales of Irish Folk Lore*. McClure, Phillips, & Co.

Moore, A. W. (1891). *The Folk-Lore of the Isle of Man: Being an Account of Its Myths, Legends, Superstitions, Customs, and Proverbs*. Brown.

Owen, E. (1896). *Welsh Folk-Lore: A Collection of the Folk-Tales and Legends of North Wales*. Woodall, Minshall, and Company.

[Registry of Donations to and Purchases from the Museum and Library, 1943-44]. (1944). National Museums of Scotland.

Rhys, J. (1901). *Celtic Folklore: Welsh and Manx*. Clarendon Press.

Scottish Fairy Tales, Folklore, and Legends. (1902). Gibbings.

Seymour, J. D. (1913). *Irish Witchcraft and Demonology*. Hodges, Figgis, & Co.

Thomas, W. J. (1908). *The Welsh Fairy Book*. T. Fisher Unwin.

Waugh, F. W. (1918). "Canadian Folk-Lore from Ontario." *The Journal of American Folklore*, 31(119), pp. 4-82.

Wilde, J. F. A. (1887). *Ancient Legends, Mystic Charms, and Superstitions of Ireland.* Tricknor and Co.

Yeats, W. B. (1888). *Fairy and Folk Tales of the Irish Peasantry.* W. Scott.

www.ingramcontent.com/pod-product-compliance
Lightning Source LLC
Chambersburg PA
CBHW020516080526
44583CB00013B/613